INHERIT THE PROMISE

INHERIT THE PROMISE

Six Keys to New Testament Thought

BY PIERSON PARKER

GREENWICH · CONNECTICUT · 1957

© 1957 by The Seabury Press, Incorporated
Library of Congress Catalogue Card Number: 57-10127
Design by Stefan Salter
Printed in the United States of America

To my sister
THEODORA SORG

PREFACE

This book is about New Testament religion. It examines six key assumptions that were in the minds of the earliest Christians, to show how these assumptions led inescapably into the faith of the New Testament and of Christianity. That faith found varieties of expression but it was, and is, one faith.

Many books have been written on New Testament literature and history for general consumption. Crucial as these are, the inquiring layman—church member or not—will ask a more basic question: What is Christianity, and why? The student in a college class in religion asks it, too. So, indeed, must the Christian minister. The author has endeavored to speak to all of these. It seems to have been the layman, however, whose figure rose most vividly before his mind as the material unfolded.

New Testament scholars will recognize on nearly every page the debt to contemporary thinkers. Not infrequently a fresh interpretation is offered (e.g., *Mark 11:12-14*) which, it is hoped, accords better than some former ones have done, with the consistent pattern of New Testament thought. Biblical quotations are made largely from the *American Revised Version*, because of its literal accuracy and its familiar language; but its readings have been altered, or departed from altogether, when this served to bring out the sense more exactly.

Profound thanks are due to the groups, clergy and lay, who listened to presentations of this material on the East and West Coasts and in the Middle West. Such value as the book may have comes largely from their gracious comment and criticism.

PIERSON PARKER

TABLE OF CONTENTS

· *ix*

CONTENTS

THE NEW TESTAMENT:

QUESTIONS AND FIRST THOUGHTS

CHAPTER I

IS THE BIBLE TRUE?

Did you ever go to a public library to borrow a book on the life of Christ? If so, and if the library is classified on the usual decimal system, you may have noticed that the number on the back of the book is 232. That number points to an interesting circumstance. In the decimal system the numbers from 230 to 239 are for books on theology, while books about the Bible are placed in the 220's. In other words Melvil Dewey, who published the system in 1876, thought that the life of Jesus should come under theological inquiry and not under history and literature of the Bible. He was not alone in thinking that. In fact the life of Jesus has been treated as a theological study, rather than a historical one, not only in the nineteenth century but ever since Christianity began.

Allied to this is another common practice. To many people the Bible, and especially the New Testament, seems useful mainly as a collection of isolated texts or short devotional passages. There are many reasons for this. Partly it comes from the way most of our Bibles are printed, with each verse given as a separate numbered paragraph. Partly it is because passages that are read in church services are necessarily short and disconnected. No doubt it is also because textbooks on Christian doctrine have so often taken passages out of their contexts and rearranged them under the topical headings of systematic theology.

There is a still more weighty reason. Many people find the Bible, or a large part of it, just too hard to understand. Take the long list of 'begats' which opens the New Testament, for instance. Or, take a sentence like this:

The beast that thou sawest was, and is not; and shall ascend out of the bottomless pit, and go into perdition: and they that dwell on the earth shall wonder, whose names were not written in the book of life from the foundation of the world, when they behold the beast that was, and is not, and yet is.

One would have to study a long time to get much out of that! The New Testament contains many such difficult passages. So the conscientious layman, and the minister too, *selects* from the Bible the parts that seem to fit his need, and he lets the rest go. The theologian sometimes uses the Bible as a collection of 'proof texts' for doctrinal formulas. The legalist finds in it a series of regulations for moral behavior or for church government.

Such practices are familiar to most of us. No doubt some of them have their value. Yet even at their best they do not make for a very intelligent use of the New Testament:[1] for *the New Testament is just not that kind of book.*

In 1835-46 David Friedrich Strauss published a *Life of Jesus.* This proved to be the beginning of a long process, not yet over, in which the New Testament, and particularly the life of our Lord, has been subjected to intensive scientific and historical study. Sometimes these studies have thrown a brilliant light on passage after passage in the New Testament, so that its contents carry new, richer, deeper meanings. At other times, however, the

[1] Or of the Old Testament either.

effect has seemed to be just the opposite. Questions have been raised and doubts have been thrown on some of our most cherished ideas about Holy Scripture.

Take for example the so-called 'literary criticism' of the Gospels: the study of their literary structure, and of how they were produced. It is now proved beyond serious doubt that both Matthew and Luke used written sources, such as the Gospel of Mark, or a lost document which we label 'Q' (from German *Quelle* = 'source'). Each Gospel author handled his materials in a different way, sometimes editing and rearranging, sometimes borrowing whole sections with little or no change from an earlier book, often adding new matter of his own. Even *Mark*, which was composed before *Matthew* or *Luke*, depended on still earlier material. *John*, on the other hand, was produced later than *Mark* or *Luke* (though perhaps not later than *Matthew*) and represents a very different point of view. The ancients had no laws of copyright; such laws were made only after the invention of printing. In the early days of Christianity it was considered quite legitimate to borrow material without acknowledgment, and to rework it according to one's own plan. The result is that the Gospels turn out to be largely 'scissors-and-paste' compilations, pieced together out of prior documents and bits of tradition of varying origin and unequal dependableness.

Another example is the century-long research into the backgrounds of Jesus' life. Today we are able to reconstruct, as our great-grandfathers could not, a great deal of the world of Jesus' day. We know much about his boyhood environment, the sort of school he would have attended, the experiences he would have had, playing beside the lake or near the great trade route that led from Egypt through Galilee and northward to Asia Minor. We can describe, with great probability, the poor little dwelling that was his childhood home. We know what books were popular and what ideas were in the Galilean air. The result is a fascinating picture, and we are able to see how hugely Jesus towered above the religion of his time. We can also see, however, in how many ways he must be recognized as a true son of his own people and century.

As a third example, consider the study of the history of religions. Analogies to New Testament religion, sometimes disturbingly close, are found in the surrounding paganism of the first century. In some Greek cults neophytes were baptized.[2] Some had sacred meals of a form that reminds us of the Christian Eucharist. When the Christian says, 'To me, to live is Christ,' or, 'Christ in you, the hope of glory,' he must recall that pagans, too, used to try to merge their lives with the life of a chosen deity. Several cultures had traditions about a dying and rising saviour god. Words of the Jewish Rabbi Hillel sound like the Golden Rule: 'Whatsoever is hateful to thee, do not to another.' In far away China, Confucius said much the same thing.

Of course, Jesus was not directly indebted to most of these, and his life and teachings again tower high above them. Yet he did draw from a heritage that contained different and often contradictory strands, from the prophets and the rabbis, and from pessimistic 'apocalyptists' who thought the world so evil that only God could intervene and set it to rights. Jesus' followers did use Greek thought-forms in trying to explain him to themselves and to their world.

Let us take, as a final instance, the modern discipline which is known in German as *Formgeschichte*, in English

[2] Not always in water, however. See below, pages 122f.

as 'form history' or 'form criticism.' This method recognizes that even our earliest known Gospel was written a full generation after Jesus' death. So form criticism tries to get behind the Gospels, to the time when stories of Jesus were simply passed from mouth to mouth. It was during that pre-Gospel period that Christianity spread over much of the Mediterranean area, and that a sharp division arose between Jewish and Gentile Christians. It must have been a highly creative period. The Church of the time surely selected, from the many stories about Jesus, the ones that best fitted its needs. Constant retelling would surely change the stories somewhat. Indeed, traditions about Jesus might even have developed right out of the life situation of the early Christians! Hence, some students feel, the *forms* in which many of the Gospel stories are told, and no little of the content too, grew out of the preaching and teaching *needs* of the early Christian community. The order of events in the Gospels, and many sayings and incidents, appear to such students to be anachronistic and suspect. Now form criticism is comparatively new, and New Testament scholars are not agreed as to how useful it really is. Certainly it is right, however, in reminding us that we ought to think about the beliefs of the earliest followers of Christ, and to try to understand on what grounds those beliefs were based.

Yet where does all this leave the Christian? The results of scientific study do seem, on their face, sharply to contradict the faith of our fathers. The problem concerns the theologian and the historian, but far more deeply it concerns every one who ever heard of Jesus. Whether I accept Christianity, or reject it, or refuse to decide, in any case I must take *some* attitude. My attitude will be determined—or ought to be—by how I think Christianity is related to the real facts.

Is the Bible true? Does it still have something urgent and at the same time *dependable* to say to an upset world?

CHAPTER II

SOME ANSWERS OF THE PAST

Science versus religion—every educated person has faced the problem. Usually the conflict has seemed to be between religion and physics, or biology, or psychology. Now, however, the dilemma appears inside Christianity itself. It seems difficult (some might say impossible) to have both a scientific study of the Bible and a simple religious faith. What is to be done? Shall we close our minds to scientific study, charge New Testament scholars with unholy motives, embrace a naïve and undiscriminating religion, and let historical research go hang? Shall we go to the other extreme, adopt a completely negative judgment about the New Testament, and say that the Jesus whom it portrays is largely a myth and very largely irrelevant to the needs of our distracted world? Or shall we suspend judgment—and thus *in effect* reject the Christian claim?

Many have taken one or another of these positions. Yet to any one who has sensed the enormous value and truth that can be got only through unprejudiced, scientific inquiry, but has also felt the power of the Christ to the depth of his being, none of these alternatives is possible. The history of Christian thought in the past century is filled with efforts to find a middle way, which should keep the values of the historic faith and at the same time allow an open highway to scholarly study. We shall here note eight such approaches. Every one of them could be documented, with quotations from a hundred years of discussion. It is not necessary to document them, however. They are all familiar.

1. *Base Christianity entirely on the authority of the Church or the Bible, or else on deductive theological reasoning.* In any case, *make scientific study subservient.* Use science when it helps to buttress our position; but when it does not, then either ignore it or explain it away.

At this point it is necessary to be absolutely clear. The Bible is, as this book itself will try to show, the Word of very God, and it speaks to our world in accents our world ought to heed. The Church does speak with authority, if for no other reason than that it has been here a long time and has learned some things that are true. The authoritative experience of the Church ought to carry weight with even the most liberal-minded Christian. Furthermore, close-knit reasoning about religion can be both stimulating and enormously convincing.

None of this gives us the right, however, to *prescribe in advance* what science must say. Yet that is just what Christian leaders have sometimes seemed to do. In the supposed interest of orthodoxy a great deal of casuistry has gone toward making the Gospels agree when in fact they do not agree, or into explaining away evidence that did not support a desired conclusion. The procedure is entirely understandable. Always, and especially in times of stress, people need some solid foundation for their faith. It takes a strong man to ride out a blizzard unhoused and unclothed. People want a home, a home moreover whose walls will not come tumbling down with each new wind of scientific fashion. Yet it simply will not do, to ground our faith—our eternal destiny—on a refusal to look at facts. That is dishonest, and dishonesty cannot inherit the Kingdom of God.[1]

The Christian, just by being a Christian, takes a risk. He risks the possibility that Jesus was not what the Church has thought, or even that Jesus never lived. This is, after all, the same kind of risk that all of us take in all our personal relationships. When a man marries, he runs the risk that his spouse may not turn out to be what he thinks. Almost certainly she will not be exactly what he expects, but nobler, more complex, more profound than he had dreamed.

The Christian's risk can be reduced. One way to reduce it is by sound historical study. As we shall try to show in later pages, to be deep in history and to study history with really open mind is to find Christianity solidly founded. Another, better way to reduce risk is through one's own personal experience of Christ. Yet the risk cannot be eliminated, and we should do ourselves no service by pretending that it can be. If someone could prove that Jesus never lived, or that he was not what Christianity thinks he was, it would make all the difference in the world. Are we afraid to face that? Then we are of poorer mettle than the apostle who wrote,

If Christ be not risen, then is our preaching vain, and your faith also vain. Yea, and we are found false witnesses of God. . . . [and] are of all men most pitiable. (*I Corinthians 15:14-19*)

It took courage to say that. It takes courage today to hazard our faith and destiny on the facts about our Lord. Without hazard, however, life would not be worth living.

[1] To say nothing of the fact that, when a conclusion is prescribed in advance, then argument for it ceases to be very persuasive or, except as an oddity, particularly interesting.

2. *There is a process sometimes called 'whittling down the records.'* If science has disproved part of the Bible, all right: lay that part aside, whittle it off. What is left may be smaller than the Bible our grandparents believed in, but at least it will be a dependable basis for religious faith. Like the first suggestion, this one rises out of sharp human need. We long for solid ground beneath our feet, and it appears better to trust a little that is sure, rather than a great deal that is not sure.

There are places where this principle can be applied with confidence. It is known, for example, that St. Paul did not write *Hebrews,* nor most of *I* and *II Timothy* and *Titus;* but that he did write *Romans, I* and *II Corinthians, Galatians* and several others. To explore St. Paul's faith, then, we may safely depend on the latter group of letters. Similarly, it is known with a high degree of certainty which parts of the Gospels are early and which late. For a true picture of Jesus it is usually better to use the documents written closest to his own lifetime.

On the other hand, when we come to *particular* incidents or sayings of Jesus or of his followers, the matter is not so simple. Of course, no honest person will cling to a passage as history if the weight of objective evidence is against it. The trouble is that one is usually caught up not by the objective evidence, but by one's own notion of what could or could not have happened. When, for example, it is concluded that Jesus did not perform a certain miracle, this is seldom because there is evidence against that particular miracle. It is, much more likely, because one has become *convinced in advance* that miracles never happen. Or when it is decided that Jesus did not say a particular thing, this *may* be because the saying is really out of keeping. But more often it is because we feel that Jesus, being a man, could not have known some things the Gospels say he knew.

Here one could easily fall into the same trap as the first group: prescribing in advance what the conclusions are to be. Of course, these conclusions, unlike the first, would be based on what one took to be the modern scientific spirit. Even so it is hard, in whittling down the records, not to be unreasonably subjective in one's decisions. In practice few definitions of the residuum have coincided very closely. That is, the process has not left a core that everybody would accept regardless of his own bias, and which might thus be made a universal religious authority.

3. *Another procedure is to 'compartmentalize': accept both science and religion but keep them separate in our minds.* Of course, this means to be inconsistent with ourselves; but who is ever completely consistent? To be that, one must either know everything or else shut out from his mind everything he does not understand.

Inconsistency runs through all our thinking. Sir Arthur Eddington once described the dilemma of the physicist in dealing with the transmission of light. In some respects light acts like continuous waves, and can be studied by the science of wave mechanics. In other respects light behaves like a series of isolated, indivisible particles or *quanta* and an altogether different principle, called quantum theory, has to be used. The two theories seem completely incompatible, yet both are necessary. Eddington said that the physicist is tempted to use one theory on Mondays, Wednesdays and Fridays, and the other on Tuesdays, Thursdays and Saturdays! [2]

[2] *The Nature of the Physical World* (New York: Macmillan, 1928), pp. 195ff.

The same temptation besets the Christian. Our finite, human minds never grasp all the truth in a single view. Sometimes a biblical scholar will write a book that seems, on the surface, to be negative and to throw out much that is precious in the Bible. Yet this very man may, on his knees, embrace a sincere and simple faith in the Lord Christ. Consciously or unconsciously, every one stresses one conviction at one time, another at another; and to many people this appears to be the only way to meet the problem.

There is another reason for our inconsistency, which will be developed in later pages. Christianity itself deals constantly with ideas that seem opposed to one another. Man is physical, yet he is spiritual too. Jesus is truly divine, yet truly human. God is an absolutely just Judge, yet He is a loving and gracious Father. God is all-powerful, yet man has free will. Christianity is like the string of a bow, which is tied at both ends and so is tugged in opposite directions. The Christian is constantly pulled in these seemingly contrary ways.

Yet if the string were tied to only one end at a time, the bow would be no bow at all. No more can the Christian find tensile strength if he ties his mind just to science at one moment, just to religion at another. Truth is one. Dividing one's mind into water-tight compartments cannot be the final way to an answer.

4. *Sometimes when faith seems to contradict modern ideas, people will try to get around it by reading into the Bible the concepts of their own age.* The Bible, they seem to say, is more up-to-date than you think. From one standpoint they are quite right. In dealing with human passions, and with good and evil, and God and man, the

Scriptures are indeed 'up-to-date,' and much of the New Testament is a long way ahead of us.

Usually, however, followers of this method have been concerned with other topics. Philo Judaeus, who lived in Egypt in the first century A.D., convinced himself that Greek philosophy was taught in the Bible (that is, in the Old Testament). Early in the twentieth century many social reformers decided that Jesus was a social reformer too. A few writers have thought they found the science of evolution in the first chapter of Genesis. One, a businessman, discovered that Jesus was an expert in modern advertising! The 'peril of modernizing Jesus' besets everybody who ever thinks about him. That is partly because we do not know all that we might, of Jesus' own life and background. Partly it comes from the fact that we honor and love him, and want to count him among ourselves.

Yet one point is surely obvious. *The only way to begin to understand our Lord is to see him, to the utmost of our ability, as he really was, and to listen to his words in the context in which he actually spoke them.* Those are the needs that give to New Testament studies (and to this book) their only reason for existence.

5. During the nineteenth and early twentieth centuries there was developed a solution which appealed to some of the world's greatest thinkers—the answer of *metaphysical idealism*. It was based largely on the teachings of Georg Wilhelm Friedrich Hegel, a German philosopher who lived from 1770 to 1831. There is much more to metaphysical idealism than can be considered here.[3] For

[3] Indeed, idealistic philosophers differ from each other rather widely. A good popular presentation of metaphysical idealism will be found in W. E. Hocking, *Types of Philosophy* (New York, Scribner's revised ed., 1939), especially chapters XIX-XXIX and XXXVII-XXXVIII.

our purposes its most important point is that *all that really exists is ideas of the mind,* our mind or the mind of God. Matter, time, human events have no independent reality of their own. They are simply the expressions or thoughts of mind. God Himself is absolute Mind. What we have, then, is a kind of one-way street, in which everything begins in mind, and issues in mental ideas like matter and history. It follows that mind can affect matter, but matter cannot affect mind! Therefore we may safely study history and science all we please. There will not be the slightest disturbance to our real relationship with God.

This point of view has found expression in some popular religious movements of today, like Christian Science, New Thought, Unity, the Science of Mind. Different as these faiths are from one another, they all say that the only *real* reality is spiritual or mental, and that matter and history are secondary, or controllable mental 'externalizations,' or insignificant, or false. In emphasizing the Holy Spirit these cults have done a great service, for the historic Church has often neglected that part of its faith. Yet neither the movements themselves nor the philosophy behind them can be called fully Christian. Full Christianity does take matter and history with utmost seriousness. More than any other religion (except perhaps Judaism) Christianity is rooted solidly in historical happenings. As we shall see, it insists on a real Incarnation, real sacraments, the real importance of the human body, and a real and visible Christian community. The things you see with your eyes and touch with your fingers are important to God. He takes them, fills them with Himself, and makes them vehicles for our knowledge of Him. In a religion based on Hegel such concepts are much weakened, or are not present at all.

6. *Some students have distinguished between what they call the religion* of *Jesus, and the religion* about *Jesus.* Behind this distinction lies an assumption. It is supposed that Jesus himself was but a simple carpenter of Galilee, though he may have been better educated than others. Somehow his soul caught fire with a message about the Fatherhood of God and the Brotherhood of Man. He went up and down the countryside preaching this message, and exemplifying it in his own life. Finally he went to martyrdom for it. His early followers were sure that his influence could never die, and some of them may even have had visions of him after his death. These were gradually crystallized into stories that he had risen from death. Then Paul, who had never known Jesus personally, got converted to Christianity. Paul was given to intense emotions and ecstatic experiences (perhaps he was an epileptic?); and besides, he had been in touch with many pagan notions about saviour gods, sacred meals and the like. Paul put all this together in an elaborate religion about Christ, one that had no sanction in Jesus' own teachings and that Jesus himself would never have acknowledged. The Church has followed not Jesus but Paul, and has thrown about Jesus' shoulders 'a heavy mantle of gold brocade' which he would have been unwilling to wear. If all or most of this is true, we shall have to be governed by it. Faced with a choice between what Jesus intended and what Paul made of it, most of us probably will vote for the religion *of* Jesus.

Yet there are huge difficulties in supposing that Paul disrupted the faith in this way. First, in his thinking about our Lord, Paul clearly was in step with those who had known Jesus personally. Paul had some sharp tiffs with other Church leaders, but never over his teachings about Christ. Nor were the early Christians afraid to attack false notions about Jesus when these actually arose. They did so on many occasions. Paul himself declared that what he taught about Christ he got from the other apostles,[4] and his teaching closely resembles what is found in many other parts of the New Testament both early and late: *Hebrews, John, I Peter, Mark,* and even the primitive *Q* source that Matthew and Luke used.[5] In *Q,* Jesus' personal claims are pressed as insistently as in anything the great apostle ever said about him:

Whosoever receiveth you receiveth me, and whosoever receiveth me receiveth him that sent me. (*Matthew 10:40 = Luke 9:48*)

He that loveth father or mother more than me is not worthy of me, and he that loveth son or daughter more than me is not worthy of me. (*Matthew 10:37 = Luke 14:26*)

Whosoever doth not take his cross and follow after me is not worthy of me. (*Matthew 10:38 = Luke 14:27*)

Not every one that saith unto me, Lord, Lord, shall enter into the kingdom of heaven. (*Matthew 7:21 = Luke 6:46*)

Every one therefore who shall confess me before men, him will I also confess before my Father who is in heaven. But whosoever shall deny me before men, him will I also deny before my Father who is in heaven. (*Matthew 10:32f. = Luke 12:8f.*)

All things have been delivered unto me of my Father: and no one knoweth the Son, save the Father neither doth any know the Father, save the Son, and he to whomsoever the Son willeth to reveal him. (*Matthew 11:27 = Luke 10:22*)

This, clearly, is religion *about* Jesus, yet it is in the heart of Jesus' own, earliest recorded words.

A further question must be asked of those who wish to

---

[4] See, for example, I Corinthians 15:1,3; Philippians 4:9; I Thessalonians 2:13,14; 4:1.
[5] Above, page 5.

separate the religion *of* Jesus from the religion *about* him. How is Jesus' own religion to be defined? If we drop everything that makes him an object of worship, still there are points that may embarrass a modern mind. He talked about angels, and demons, and the end of the world, and Jewish ceremonies. He was deeply troubled about the fate of his own nation. If those things no longer concern us, presumably they too should be put to one side. Then there will be left, let us say, Jesus' awareness that God is Father, his great ethical teachings, his example of faithfulness to his task. These are splendid things, certainly—provided we can extricate them from their discarded contexts. Still, when we compare them with stories from the Old Testament, or from India or China, or from our own land, they seem hardly new or distinctive.

Other phrases are sometimes used, to point up the supposed difference between what Jesus wanted and what the Church has believed: 'the Jesus of history and the Christ of faith,' 'the Jesus-or-Paul controversy.' The issue is, of course, whether there was such a 'controversy' or not. Those who think that there was should be prepared to say just what Jesus' own religion included; how it is identified as really his; why his friends became so excited about it; and why it should be considered binding on us now.

7. Some writers have tried to meet this last demand. *Jesus' explicit teachings, it is said, are pretty irrelevant to our later age.* As a child of his time he shared all that mass of primitive ideas and impressions that have since been discarded. Behind his specific words and acts, however, was a *spirit*. It is that spirit that we must try to reflect in our own tormented world. Sometimes his state of mind is described as a 'reverence for personality.' No

doubt Jesus had that. No doubt we need it too. Once more, however, in what way is this attitude *peculiar to him?* and how can we separate his spirit from what he himself did and said and was?

8. The final proposal we shall consider, here, is the recommendation that *we find the central key to Jesus' ministry, and concentrate on that.* From one standpoint it is just what we ought to do. It is of the nature of greatness, and supremely of Jesus' own stupendousness, that he should be dominated by one controlling purpose. Yet to pick out what was really his central theme, to be able to say, 'This, and not something else, was *the* great impulse of his life,' has proved far from easy. Here again, our decision is easily affected by what we *want* to believe about him. Mr. A will find that Jesus was chiefly a great teacher of morals; Mr. B, that he was a sublime poet and story-teller; Mr. C, that he was most of all a healer who 'went about doing good,' or a rabbi, or a political reformer, or even a seer whose understanding of the future had discernible limits. Whatever the choice, it has often meant that major parts of the Gospels are ignored, or declared untrustworthy, for the sole reason that they do not fit the chosen interpretation.

In listing these efforts to mediate between scientific criticism and religious faith, we must not be blind to two facts. In the first place, every one of them stems from profound and sincere religious motives. The dilemma really does exist. In trying to solve it some of the world's best thinkers and most deeply religious men have—at least for a time—adopted one or another of the above positions.

In the second place, nearly every one of these points of view contains an important truth. Christianity *ought* to be able to speak with authority. We do have to emphasize now one aspect of religion, now another, because we do not grasp it whole and all at once. God *is* Spirit, and is to be worshipped in spirit and in truth. Parts of the New Testament *are* anachronistic or otherwise questionable. We *are* concerned to understand Jesus' central purpose and to interpret it to our own age.

Nevertheless, it is safe to say that none of the foregoing approaches, nor any combination of them, has long commended itself as a final solution, to more than a handful of thinkers. The reason can be quickly stated. *These compromises simply do not account for the terrific impact that Jesus made on those who knew him best.* Jesus had to be great enough to do what he did.

To put it another way, if Jesus was as restricted as some people think, why did his followers ever choose *him* for the focal center of their religion? Remember that these followers were native-born Jews, who had been taught from earliest childhood that God is One alone. Most of them were, in addition, Galileans who all their lives had supposed that Messiah would come as a warlike king. Further, these men knew Jesus very well (outwardly, at least). They had lived, traveled, eaten, preached, and slept out under the stars in his company, for perhaps three years. There could be few better ways to learn to know some one, and to come under his spell. It was not Paul but Peter, one of this early, intimate group, who was so overwhelmed that he fell at Jesus' feet and cried, 'Depart from me, for I am a sinful man, O Lord.' Later, Peter said to Jesus, 'Thou art the Messiah.' Still later, in the face of arrest and persecution, Peter demanded publicly, 'Let all the house of Israel understand beyond a doubt that God hath made him both Lord and Messiah, this Jesus whom ye crucified!'

What was it about Jesus, that affected Peter and the others in this way? That is a religious question, but it is a scholarly, historical question too. Only by answering it can we begin to bridge the gap between scientific, biblical criticism and the ancient faith.

CHAPTER III

FINDING A BETTER ANSWER

In the middle years of the twentieth century, biblical research turned a corner. For a hundred years scholars had been studying the archeology, history, language and literature of Bible times. Now there was added a new interest, a new approach toward *interpreting* the Bible's meaning. Books began to appear with titles such as, *An Outline of Biblical Theology, Theological Word Book of the Bible, New Testament Thought, Theologisches Wörterbuch zum Neuen Testament* ('Theological Dictionary for the New Testament'), while scores of others, with less transparent names, offered fresh understandings of the Bible's deep religious insights.

At first the new studies were concerned chiefly with the Old Testament. This was natural. Much of the Old Testament was written in times of war, and of cracking civilizations, so that its mood appealed to the sombre twentieth-century mind. Soon, however, the religion of the New Testament also came in for fresh scrutiny, and scholars found themselves on the threshold of a new era, a new New Testament theology.

Of course, people have been interpreting and explaining New Testament religion ever since the earliest Christian book was written. So it is important to see both what this new New Testament theology is not, and what it is.

First of all, it is not a repetition of the methods which we looked at in the last chapter. Certainly we must keep what is true and useful in those procedures; but the new approach was made for the very reason that the older explanations did not explain.

Second, it is not a mere comparing of New Testament religion with other faiths. One can, of course, find analogies to other religions in this or that part of the New Testament. It has been done many times. We can, and ought to, consider the backgrounds of New Testament faith and the sources from which it came. Yet these are something like trying to understand an oak by studying *only* the acorn, or a lily by examining *only* the soil in which it grew. The lily is not the mire. The oak is not an acorn—nor is the oak just like any other tree. It is the *different* quality of New Testament religion that sets it off from everything else, and that makes it the most powerful, most indestructible force the world has ever seen.

Third, it is not just a fresh gathering of Bible passages to support some chosen belief. True enough, one can find verses, many verses, to fit every clause of the Apostles' or the Nicene Creed. But then, by careful picking and choosing one could find verses to fit other creeds too —Jewish or Unitarian or Christian Scientist or Mormon. That is not surprising. The Bible was written over many centuries, and touches almost every phase of human experience. With so much variety, it is almost certain to have some sentence, tucked away somewhere, that sounds like almost any idea we might name.[1] This is not to say that 'proof texts' are always objectionable. At times they

---

[1] Of course the sentence would have to be taken out of context, and given a meaning its author did not intend. But that is just what people have sometimes done, even people who should know better.

can be quite valuable. Unless they are chosen with care
and understanding, however, they can prove a waste of
time or worse. The new New Testament theology deals
not with isolated texts but with the total impact of each
book, and the total impact of the whole New Testament.

In fact the new New Testament theology seeks answers
to two very definite questions.

1. *What did these writers see?* Why did they think
that with Jesus' coming a new age had dawned in the
history of the world? What kind of new age did they think
it was? What was it about Jesus that made them call him
Lord, Messiah, Second Adam, Lamb of God, Heavenly
Priest, King of kings?

Now *what* the early Christians believed, and *why* they
believed it, are matters of objective, historical fact. Yet
facts like these cannot be fully brought out by the scientific methods that had prevailed for over a century. Some
one has said that you can tell as much about a man from
the lies that are told about him as from the truth: for
he must be the kind of man of whom such lies could be
told, and be believed. So it is not enough to know that
one New Testament book was written early, another
late; or that this passage is more authentic than that
one. Conceivably, a true story might be told in such a
way as to give a miserably distorted impression; while
another story, with not a shred of fact behind it, might
still be brilliantly characteristic of our Lord and faithful
to his meaning and purpose.

This may be made clearer by an illustration. Suppose
we were trying to gauge the character of a medieval
nobleman, from a portrait of him done in oils. Of course,

it would be useful to know who and how skilful the artist was, and whether he was disposed to idealize his subject or to exaggerate blemishes. We should like to know whether he painted from life, or from memory, or from another portrait. We should like to know what kind of art was fashionable in those days, and even the sorts of paint and brushes that were used. Yet helpful as such information would be, something else is far more valuable. To understand the nobleman, and what he meant to the one who knew him, *we must stand back and look at the picture!*

The new New Testament theology is a disciplined effort to stand back and look at the picture, to see what the earliest Christians saw and, so far as possible, through their eyes. For this there must be a new method, a different set of criteria, from those that biblical studies formerly used. Here, let it be repeated, is no decrying of the older scientific procedures. Indeed the new discipline would not have been possible without the century of spade-work that preceded it. That spade-work is not finished, and will not be for a very long time. When new questions come, however, new ways must be found to answer them.

2. The second question is a semantic one: *How can we, with the least possible distortion, translate New Testament ideas into the language and thought-forms of today?*

Peoples' backgrounds and cultures differ, and there is hardly a term, in any language, that has an exact equivalent in any other. Even so simple a word as *chair* will carry a different set of meanings to an American from what *Stuhl* means to a German, or *chaise* to a Frenchman, or *yü-tsze* to a Shanghai Chinese. (Try translating, 'The president took the chair,' or 'The chair of English at the University,' or, 'I have a seat in the chair car,' into any of these languages.) If this is true of concrete objects, it is still more true of abstract ideas. It is most true of all in religion. The word *Christ* or *Messiah*, for example, will evoke one response in the orthodox Christian's mind, steeped in two thousand years of Christian tradition; another for the 'left-wing liberal'; still another for the Jew.[2] All of these differ, again, from the thought of the earliest disciples whose beloved little land was under the heel of Rome, and who longed for a Messiah to set their nation free.

Therefore it is not enough to take the ancient word and spell it in our alphabet, M-e-s-s-i-a-h. It is not enough to know that *Messiah* is from a Hebrew root, *Christ* from a Greek root, both of which mean *Anointed One*. It is not even enough, to know what Christ has meant to sixty generations of Christians. The New Testament faith is itself the rock from which all Christianity is hewn. To understand, and explain to our age, the meaning of this faith, we must find out what the New Testament writers themselves were thinking about when they wrote of the Messiah; or of the Lord, or the Kingdom, or the Church, or all the other terms they used to declare their conviction.

One way to do this would be to take each word separately and examine it. That has sometimes been done, and it is a most useful thing.[3] Yet behind the various

[2] And does not each of the words, *Christ* and *Messiah*, produce a somewhat different response in your own mind? Yet originally they were intended to convey the same meaning.

[3] An excellent example is *A Theological Word Book of the Bible*, edited by Alan Richardson (New York: Macmillan, 1951). The most monumental work of this sort is *Theologisches Wörterbuch zum Neuen Testament*, begun by Gerhard Kittel and continued by Gerhard Friedrich. Some articles from the latter have been published in English under the title *Bible Key Words* (London: Adam and Charles Black; New York: Harper, 1951-52).

words lay a culture, a nation's history, and a whole way of thinking about the world and about God. Excellent as it is to define a set of words, it is still more essential *to know what kind of thinking called those words forth.*

This will be our task in the pages that follow: to put ourselves back into the first century and, in particular, to see the world of a Palestinian Jew through his eyes. Then we may begin to see what Jesus of Nazareth really did to that world.

THE FIRST KEY:

THE IDEA OF THE COVENANT

CHAPTER IV

THE OLD COVENANT

Every person takes over from his environment a huge set of ideas, or ways of thinking about life. Some of these may be trivial: what clothes to wear, what slang is fashionable, what kinds of behavior are socially acceptable, and so on. Other ideas are by no means trivial. What do we believe about individual responsibility, or group life, or the profit motive, or personal integrity? What goals do we consider worth striving for? What place has God in our thinking, and what kind of God is He? The people's *real attitudes* to those things will affect their nation's entire destiny. Yet unless some one challenges them, most of our ideas are held quite unconsciously. They are all around us, like the air we breathe. Without thinking about them very much, we just live from day to day as though they were true.

The Jew of Jesus' day was like that. His mind was permeated with certain basic concepts which he had absorbed from earliest childhood. His parents had learned these ideas from their parents, and they from theirs, and on back through fourteen centuries of history. Therefore, to understand the minds of Jesus' followers, we must first understand something of their nation's past.

Throughout the Orient, and particularly throughout the Near East, run two great correlative ideas, *the community* and *group responsibility*. The ancient Hebrew shared these ideas.[1] He thought of himself not just as a private person but as a kind of cell in the ongoing life of his family, tribe or nation. When disaster came it would often be less dismaying than to a modern Westerner, since the Hebrew knew that he was part of the larger whole. He would take the long view over past and coming ages. His moral duty was not his alone; it was shared by his group. He looked for his reward not just in his own comfort and fortune, but in the life of his descendants. So the greatest gift that could come to Abraham was the promise, 'In thy seed [i.e., descendants] shall all the nations of the earth be blessed.' [2]

These attitudes had their darker side. A whole family, or a whole tribe, could be punished for a crime committed by one of its members. There was, for a long time, no clear idea of life beyond death, so that rewards and punishments were thought to be limited to the present, physical world. Even so, the ancient Hebrew has much to teach the modern Westerner. The Westerner would not lose by realizing, more fully than he sometimes does, how intimately his life is bound up with the life of his people, his forebears and the generations still to come. To take the long view, to see one's life as part of a totality, to

[1] Some people are confused over the various names *Hebrew, Israelite* and *Jew*. *Hebrew* was the generic or racial name of these people. *Israel* was another name for Abraham's grandson Jacob. It was applied to the people because, reputedly, their twelve tribes were descended from Jacob's twelve sons. When the nation split in two after Solomon's death, 'Israel' was the specific name of the northern kingdom. However, it is still applied to the whole group of people, and will be so used in this book.

After the split the southern kingdom, comprising the two tribes of Judah and Benjamin, was called 'Judah,' and from this comes the word *Jew*. (Except for the division between north and south, tribal distinctions were largely theoretical.)

The modern nation of Israel is descended from the southern kingdom.
[2] Genesis 12:3; 17:6f.; Galatians 3:13ff.

learn to say and mean 'we'—these are the conditions of emotional and religious maturity.

While the ideas of community and group responsibility are widespread in the Orient, they find their most intensive and lasting expression in the pages of the Old Testament. And there they are pervaded by, and subsumed under, an idea that is greater still. It is *the idea of the Covenant.*

Say 'covenant' to an average modern, and it will mean little to him. He may think of a contract, or a secret society, or (if he is an active Protestant) of a group of people 'covenanting' together to form a church congregation. Yet none of these may occur to him, for the word is seldom used nowadays. And none of them fits the meaning of *Covenant* in the Bible.

Before we see what the biblical word means, one caution is necessary. We shall speak of Moses and Abraham, of Noah and Adam. However, we are not now asking what really happened to these men, but what people afterward *thought* had happened. Perhaps you believe every word of the Bible literally. Perhaps, on the contrary, you doubt that Moses and the others ever existed at all. *For our present purposes that does not matter.* What does matter is the terrific influence that Covenant thinking had on nearly every writer from the earliest story-teller of *Genesis* to the last great seer of *Revelation.* This is what they believed:

The Hebrew people had been in slavery, in Egypt. Year by year, under one Pharaoh (Egyptian king) after another, the oppression had grown worse. Finally the Lord God commanded Moses to lead his people away. In a dreadful night the Angel of Death struck down all the first-born sons of the Egyptians. The Hebrews had sprinkled lambs' blood on the door-posts of their homes for a sign, and the Angel of Death *passed* them *over*. (The Jewish Passover is an annual celebration of that night.) In terror Pharaoh bade the Hebrews go, and Moses led them out into the desert. At the foot of Mt. Sinai they paused. In the thunderings from Sinai's peak they were sure they heard the voice of the Lord God. Moses climbed the mountain, and spoke with the Lord God. Then he descended, and he and his people made *covenant* with this God, who from henceforth was to be the God of Israel. The people did not know, then, that He is the only God at all; but He was *their* only God. They chose Him. He chose them, a total people to be in league with Him and to be His arm in the world. Henceforth Israel and her God must live, work, fight together within the bonds of an unbreakable relationship.

So binding was this Covenant that it was likened to marriage. Indeed, Hosea and Jeremiah drew from that figure some of their deepest religious lessons. God yearns over, loves and knows His people—the very verbs are those used for the relationship of husband and wife. (Such verbs may offend us, but they did not offend the ancient and franker Israelites. They put into parable what is, after all, the whole purpose of religion: *complete* communion with God.) When Israel quit her Lord and went after other gods, her defection carried all the disgrace of a wife's faithlessness to her husband.

It is no strange thing for a nation to believe itself especially chosen of God. Japanese call themselves 'Sons of Heaven,' Chinese 'the Middle Kingdom' around which others are to circle and pay tribute. Germans called themselves 'Herrenvolk,' while Americans think they know which is 'God's country.' Israel believed, however, that God had made specific promises to her—promises that she was to have not just a special place but *the* supreme place among the nations. Today we can see how truly Israel did become supreme. No nation has given more to the world, has more deeply influenced human history, or has taught mankind so much about God. Those, however, were not the kinds of greatness the Israelites expected or wanted. They wanted political power and prestige, and wealth, and to be the capital of the world with all other nations paying envious homage. Those things, so they believed, were what the God of Israel meant by His promise. Then, if Israel was bound by the Covenant, Israel's God was bound too.

The centuries brought bitter, grinding disappointment. True, Israel captured the 'promised land' of Palestine (it was called Canaan at first). But Israel in her turn felt the lash of other conquerors. These came not because Israel was important. It was not, to them. Israel produced few great statesmen, and almost no philosophers. Her land was not rich or economically powerful. It had almost no harbors. The trouble was simply that Palestine was *there* —there where it formed the shortest route between three continents. If war broke out between Africa and Asia, or Asia and Europe, or Europe and Africa, in every case Palestine must be overrun.

Five times it happened—five major times, but with countless smaller invasions between. Assyria, then Babylonia, Persia, Greece and Rome went through the land, burning its crops, razing its towns, murdering its women and children, dragging their husbands and fathers behind chariots through the streets, deporting masses of the people into captivity. This, to the people whom God had promised greatness and glory! Nearly every page of the Old Testament was wrung out of the cry of that people: *Why?*

They found five answers. These answers did not come easily or all at once. They were hammered out slowly on the anvil of Israel's torture. When the answers came, not all the people believed them. But their prophets believed, and they wrote the answers down.

1. They learned about *holiness*. The word *holy* means 'set apart' to God. Like all ancient people, the Israelites had thought of holiness in physical terms. One became holy by touching a holy object; or one ate holy food, and the holiness went down into the stomach and out to the fingers, toes and hair, until one was holy all over. Sometimes holiness was very inconvenient, for to be set apart meant that one could not go about one's daily business. Too much holiness could be positively dangerous, as when Uzzah touched the holy Ark to steady it, and was killed for his pains.[3]

Then came Isaiah, the son of Amoz. Here was one of the greatest men Israel ever produced. He was a great poet, though really to appreciate his poetry one must know Hebrew. He was a statesman. Greatest of all, he was a theologian. Isaiah discovered that *with God, holiness and righteousness are the same thing.*

He expressed it very simply. 'Cease to do wrong. Learn to do right.' With all its simplicity it was nearly the longest single stride that Israel ever took, in her thinking about God. It meant that holiness is not just physical, it is ethical. God requires of His people simple, downright, elementary goodness. God's Covenant promises would not, could not be fulfilled until Israel responded with all her soul to the unspeakable goodness of her God.

[3] II Samuel 6:3-7. Originally the words *holy* and *tabu* meant the same thing: reserved for the exclusive use of the god, and not to be touched by ordinary mortals.

2. They learned about *the power of God*. Over and over in the Old Testament one meets the phrase, 'the Day of the Lord.' That phrase tells of Israel's conviction that God's purpose cannot be forever frustrated. The Day would come when God would intervene to punish His foes,[4] and to establish His Covenant finally and for ever. All the machinations of Assyria, Babylonia, Persia, Greece or Rome, all the stupid evil of men and nations—these are as dust in the balance beside His almighty power. When Assyria was running amok, Isaiah cried: 'Holy, holy, holy is the Lord of hosts. The whole earth is full of His glory.' Later, when the Jews were being persecuted and murdered because they would not give up their faith, they sang of their God, 'His kingdom is an everlasting kingdom, and of His reign there shall be no end.'

Still later when the *Christian* Church faced its first broadside persecution and Christians were starved and beaten for refusing to worship the Emperor's image, the seer of Patmos wrote, 'The kingdoms of the world are become the kingdom of our Lord, and of His Christ, and He shall reign for ever and ever.' [5] When barbarians were knocking at the gates of Rome, the Christians sang,

We praise Thee, O God. We acknowledge Thee to be the Lord.
All the earth doth worship Thee, the Father everlasting.

And when Jesus of Nazareth was on trial for his life he could say, 'Ye shall see the Son of man sitting at the right hand of Power, and coming on the clouds of heaven' (*Mark 14:62*).

---

[4] Israel's enemies were thought of quite naturally as enemies of Israel's God. People today feel much the same way about their country's foes; but it was more intense then, because a nation's god was closely identified with the nation itself.

[5] Isaiah 6:3; Daniel 4:3; Revelation 11:15.

Thus there is a perversity about the religion of Israel, and a similar perversity about Christianity. When the world seems to crack, and civilization goes to pot, that has always been the time that Judaism and Christianity have found their strength again. If the world has been wrong about these religions, it has been just as wrong about itself. Men outside the faith may think that all is lost. Christianity knows better. Israel knew better. Not Assyria or Rome, not Russia or America, but God alone is really in control. God is Sovereign.

3. They learned about *the Messiah*—not all about him, but a great deal. Since God is good and faithful, and His sovereign power is to be trusted, then, so Israel believed, He would fulfil His promise by sending His Anointed One. This Anointed One, this Messiah, would in God's name set the world right again.

Neither the people nor their prophets agreed about who Messiah was to be. Some thought he would be an angel, others a man. Many thought he would be of their own race, and probably a descendant of King David. Others thought he might be a Gentile. So Cyrus the Persian, Alexander the Greek, and Augustus the Roman were all, in turn, called Messiah by some one. Again, the people were not of one mind as to what Messiah would do. Some held that he would bless all the nations, others that Israel alone would benefit. Some believed that he would destroy the present world and set up a new heaven and earth; others, that he would cleanse and purify this one and make Jerusalem its capital.

Yet through all these differences ran one deepening and unshakable conviction. God would keep His covenanted promise. He would do it by sending His Blessed and Elect One, His Messiah, His Christ.

4. They learned *what suffering can mean*. To the Israelite, as to other ancient people, pain was punishment. If you suffered, this showed that God was displeased with you—or else with your relatives, since punishment was often inflicted on the culprit's family and descendants. *The Book of Job* deals with this belief. Job's 'friends' are sure he must have offended God severely, to have to undergo such loss of property, family and health. Job is sure he has done no such thing and he exclaims, 'Miserable comforters are ye all!' Job's own final explanation of suffering is not much better, however: God does as He pleases, and man should not ask why. The standard theory continued to be that grief is a penalty which God exacts for wrongdoing. Even some early followers of Christ could ask merely, 'Who sinned, this man or his parents, that he should be born blind?' (*John 9:2*)

Yet centuries before Christianity a nobler understanding had been reached. We do not know the name of the man who found it. His poems became attached to the Book of Isaiah, and he is sometimes called *Deutero-* or 'the second Isaiah,' though he lived two centuries after Isaiah himself. This unknown prophet of the Exile looked back over the long story of his people's agony (he could not know how long it was still to be!) and he drew a picture of the Suffering Servant of the Lord. You can read about the Suffering Servant in what is now Isaiah 40-55, and particularly in Chapter 53. As you read these poems, two questions may come to your mind.

First, what *is* the value of pain as the prophet sees it? Plainly it is no mere expiation to an angry deity. Still less is it useless agony, ground out by a heedless universe. Suffering can be *for others*. That is the great lesson which the prophet proclaims. If we go further, however, and ask *in what way* one man's grief can help another, the prophet is not so clear. Like others in his nation, he was not a philosopher but an observer. He recorded, in some of the world's most exalted lines, what he saw. We of today see the same thing constantly. I commit a thoughtless, evil act that hurts some one I love. Then I see what my deed has cost him and I am led to remorse, and to reform. A man rushes into the street to save a child from being run over, and himself is struck. A nation's freedom is bought with the pain and death of men on a battlefield. In such countless ways pain can, indeed, be vicarious.

Perhaps we see, too, that a law of the universe is involved here. When I do wrong it is no mere offense against another human being. To strike against a creature is to strike against his Creator. Every wrong act is an act against God. But in a universe of law and balance, my evil act cannot go unbalanced. If I will not or cannot offset it, then someone else must.[6]

How much of this was in the prophet's mind we cannot tell. He saw a fact, a truth. The grief of God's Servant aids others besides the griever:[7]

> All we like sheep have gone astray.
> We have turned, every one to his own way,
> And the Lord hath laid on him the iniquity of us all.

Second, whom did the author mean by 'Suffering Servant?' Many modern scholars think he meant the nation of Israel. Some ancient Jews thought so, too. Certainly his words fit this uncouth, dejected little people:

> He hath no form nor comeliness, and when we see him
> There is no beauty, that we should desire him.

[6] This line of reasoning may be carried still further. Since all sin is sin against God, all sin is actually infinite in its consequences. Then only the infinite God is able to offset it—pay for it, balance it, expiate it. Then unless God has done so, through His Son for example, our sins remain unpaid for. Is this argument sound?

[7] This and the next two quotations are from Isaiah 53.

He was despised and rejected of men,
A man of sorrows, and acquainted with grief.
And as one from whom men hide their face
He was despised; and we esteemed him not.

If this meant Israel, then the prophet had a clear answer to the questions, why has the Covenant promise been delayed, and why has Israel undergone so much? She has suffered not for her own sake only, but for the sake of all the nations.

Other scholars believe, however, that the author was thinking of an individual, who was still to come. This individual would personify the whole people. All their hopes and heartaches would be focused in him, reënacted in him, but more, embodied in him. He would suffer as Israel had done, for in a profound sense he would *be* all of Israel 'rolled into one.' He would go down to seeming defeat. Then he would come to victory:

When thou shalt make his soul an offering for sin,
He shall see his seed, he shall prolong his days,
And the pleasure of the Lord shall prosper in his hand.
He shall see of the travail of his soul, and be satisfied:
By the knowledge of himself shall my righteous servant justify
    many:
And he shall bear their iniquities.
Therefore will I divide him a portion with the great,
And he shall divide the spoil with the strong.

This is how the Christian Church has always interpreted the prophet's words. The Suffering Servant of the Lord is an individual. In himself he embodies, and brings to fruit, the whole meaning and purpose of God and His Covenant. That individual, says the Church, is Jesus of Nazareth. Whether the Church is right, and whether Jesus himself would have chosen or allowed this interpretation, are questions we must ask in later pages.

5. Finally, through Covenant thinking Israel learned that *her God is the only God,* not just for Israel but for all the world. At first He was thought to be one among many gods, for each nation had its own. He had a personal name, *Jahveh* or *Yahweh.*[8] Amos, the first prophet to leave a book, concluded that if Israel turned faithless to Yahweh, He might choose another people. This was the first, tentative step toward recognizing that Yahweh might be interested in others besides Israel. Later, the authors of *Deuteronomy* saw that He is the greatest of the gods, indeed had appointed other gods to their respective nations. Jeremiah almost, but not quite, said that He is the only God at all. It remained for 'Deutero-Isaiah,' the same who wrote of the Suffering Servant, to declare that there is just one God. He announced this as though it were a brand new insight—which it was.

This growing understanding is seen in another way. The Covenant itself was pushed farther and farther back in time. Obviously, the earlier one dated the Covenant the more descendants one took in. At first it was thought the Covenant began with Moses. This would cover only the descendants of the Hebrews in the desert. Then it was dated with Abraham. This would (or could) cover not only Israel but related peoples too. Still later it was dated with Noah, taking in the descendants of every one

[8] No one knows how this name was pronounced, because from early times it was thought too sacred to utter. The Hebrew alphabet originally had no vowels, so that the name was written, in Hebrew letters, JHVH. When the reader came to this, he said 'the Lord' instead. Later when vowels were added, the sacred name was given the vowels *-e-o-a-,* but these were from the Hebrew word for 'Lord,' and merely reminded the reader to say 'Lord' there. Moderns did not understand this at first, so they produced the hybrid word *Jehovah* and this got into some English translations of the Bible. It is ugly ('Jehovah is my Shepherd. . . .') and has no legitimate origin. Still, it has become part of the English language and probably will remain so.

who survived the Flood. Finally it was dated with Adam, who fathered the whole human race.

The highest reach of the Old Testament is not in *Deutero-Isaiah* but in *Jonah*. This is no mere fairy tale about a whale (and it was not a 'whale' but a 'big fish'). It is the story of the prophet Jonah, ordered by the Lord to preach salvation to the Ninevites. The Ninevites were hated enemies. Jonah did not want them saved, and he tried not to go. While running away from God's demand he got thrown off a ship, swallowed by the 'whale,' and then coughed up on the very shores of Nineveh. Some time afterward Jonah planted a gourd, for shade, but the gourd withered. Then the Lord spoke to him, in words that express the Old Testament's noblest understanding of the love of God, a love that embraces all men, all children, and even beasts!

Thou hast had regard for the gourd, for which thou hast not labored, neither madest it grow; which came up in a night, and perished in a night: and should not I have regard for Nineveh, that great city, wherein are more than six score thousand persons that cannot discern between their right hand and their left hand; and also much cattle? (*Jonah 4:10-11*)

So Israel's faith grew. Rising out of the mire of surrounding polytheism and superstition, it increased and burgeoned until it became a vast and dizzying vista of the ways of God. Through all the changes one conviction did not change, and it is the heart of Covenant thinking: God works with man by and through a holy people, a *whole people*, whom He has chosen and who have chosen Him.

CHAPTER V

THE NEW COVENANT

When people meet a strange idea, they try to interpret it by what they already know. Show a man a new color, or kind of cake, or make of car, and immediately he will think, 'It is like this-or-that, but has a touch of so-and-so,' naming colors, tastes or other qualities that he has met before. We understand today's experience by linking it with yesterday's. We note what is new, and what remains unchanged.

Now the Old Testament was Jesus' Bible, and it continued to be the Christians' only Bible for a long time. That Bible turned, as we have seen, on the idea of the Covenant. Thus Covenant thinking was dominant in the Jewish mind of Jesus' day, as it has been dominant ever since. (Jews today call themselves *B'nai B'rith*, 'sons of the Covenant.') Therefore we should expect the early Christians, especially Jewish Christians, to relate their new faith to the lofty ideas they inherited from the old. They would believe that God works by means of a Covenant made between Himself as one Partner and a total people as the other. They would consider this Covenant binding, as marriage is binding. Indeed they would bring to Christianity all those thoughts about God, His purpose, and man's moral nature, that they had learned or absorbed from Israel's past.

One factor might, at first, tempt us to discount the importance of that background. At least two centuries had gone by between the last book of the Old Testament and the first book of the New. In that time much had happened, which would affect a Jew's way of looking at the world. Since 300 B.C. Palestine had been in contact with Greek civilization. Under the Greeks, and still more under the Romans, Jews migrated from Palestine and settled all over the Mediterranean area. In Jesus' day more Jews lived outside Palestine than in it. The Greek language was spoken everywhere, and those who learned it were bound to pick up some of its flavor and its cultural setting. Greek was not, indeed, the chief language of Jesus and his earliest followers; they spoke Aramaic, a tongue about as close to Hebrew as English is to Dutch. Yet Aramaic itself had taken over a good many Greek words, like *philosoph* (philosopher), *moré* (you fool), *evangelion* (gospel).[1] A few Jews, who dwelt outside Palestine, had been so influenced by Greek ways of thinking that they tried to synthesize Greek philosophy and Hebrew religion.[2] In time Christians would try the same thing. Might it not be, then, that Greek thought also weighed heavily in the Palestine of Jesus' day?

No, it can have had little real effect. The fact is that most Palestinian Jews heartily rejected all Gentile points of view. In 168 B.C. a misguided foreign king, Antiochus Epiphanes, had tried to force Greek culture and religion on the Jews. He used fire, pillage and crucifixion to persuade them, but they resisted. They offered their lives by the thousands to defend the ancient faith. They won, and in winning gained for the last time the independence of

[1] In the second century, Jewish opponents of Christianity used to make a play on the word *evangelion*. In Aramaic, *evan-gilayon* means 'a worthless thing of a book.'

[2] Compare what was said about Philo Judeus, page 15 above.

their country. When that was lost again, their hatred of Gentiles continued to burn. It burned most hotly in Galilee, where Jesus and his disciples lived and worked.

Therefore the burden of proof is on those who would say that Jesus or his first followers thought, or spoke, in other than Hebrew-Jewish ways. If the new religion went beyond the old, still, to make himself understood at all, Jesus *had* to talk in language that his Jewish hearers knew. So did his first followers. The presumption is clearly on the side of the Old Testament, as the dominant heritage in their thinking. The earliest Christians were bound to think in Covenant terms, that is, in terms of a total community in its relationship to God; and of what such a relationship implied.

So much for *a priori* expectations. When we turn to the New Testament itself, we find these expectations borne out by the most abundant and convincing evidence. The fact is that Christian Covenant thinking is just as strong in writings addressed to Gentiles as in those concerned with Jews. The apostles turned to the Old Testament right from the beginning, and they kept turning to it. Read, for example, the summaries of Christian sermons in the first part of *Acts*.[3] These are not verbatim reports, of course, for there were no stenographers to take them down; but they do reproduce the substance of the earliest Christian preaching. In every case the speaker begins by recounting for his hearers the history of Israel under the Covenant, and then goes on to show how Jesus fulfils Israel's long hope.

Or study the Old Testament quotations in the New Testament. Plainly, the Christians were finding new and

[3] For example, Acts 2:14-36; 3:12-26; 8:27-35; 13:16-41; 18:28; also St. Stephen's defense before the Jewish rulers, 7:2-53.

thrilling meanings in their beloved Scriptures. Passage after passage (like those we quoted in Chapter IV) reminded them of events in Jesus' life. Many of the passages had not before been connected with the Messiah, but the Christians became convinced that they were indeed predictions about him, the fulfiller of God's promise to Israel. So they made collections of Old Testament verses, to be used in their propaganda. Such collected passages (modern scholars call them *testimonia*, which is Latin for 'evidence of witnesses') were available, apparently, to the authors of *Matthew, John, Acts* and *Hebrews*.

Covenant thinking is seen again in the titles which New Testament writers applied to Jesus:

Suffering Servant, the figure who, as we saw, typified and embodied Israel's history.

Second Adam. The first Adam had founded the race and, so later Old Testament writers thought, was the one through whom the Covenant was made.

Heavenly Priest who offers a permanent sacrifice. Ever since 600 B.C. Judaism had had just one Temple. It was located in Jerusalem and was for the whole nation. Sacrifices for the nation were offered in the Temple every day. So when Jesus is called 'Heavenly Priest' it means that his sacrifice is for a whole people. Indeed, the author of *Hebrews* says just that.[4]

Lamb of God, himself the victim offered in sacrifice. On that first Passover night in Egypt, lamb's blood had been the sign that protected the entire Hebrew community from the Angel of Death.

Word of God (in Greek, *logos*). A Greek might have understood this in philosophical terms, as a kind of emanation from the Deity. To a Jew, however, 'Word of God'

[4] See Hebrews 6:13-10:25, but especially chapter 9.

· 47

meant the heart of the Old Testament, viz., the Mosaic Law which proclaimed God's will for man. That Law was the backbone, the constitution of the people of Israel.

Most important of all, *Messiah* or *Christ,* the fruition of Israel's hope.

We shall have occasion to discuss these titles again.[5] Notice now, however, that (1) every one of them has roots in the Old Testament. (2) *Every one of them depict Jesus as* in some way *embodying and fulfilling the meaning and purpose of a whole people.* For Jesus to appropriate these titles, or for his followers to apply them to him, meant that he was set at the climax of that people's destiny, at the climax of God's act through and for Israel.

But now there was posed for the Christians a problem, one so shocking that it must be called a catastrophe. Through fourteen centuries Israel had been God's agent, His arm in the world. During all that time, and especially in later centuries, Israel had longed for God to complete her destiny and bring in the Messiah's kingdom. Yet when Messiah came, Israel rejected him! Nothing, in all the Old Testament, had prepared Jesus' followers for that. Can we at this late date sense their confusion, their dismay at this tragic turn of events?

Opponents of Christianity could and did argue that Israel's very rejection disproved Jesus' claim. Had he been genuine, they said, the Jews could not possibly have refused him. To the Christian, however, Jesus' resurrection was enough, by itself, to prove that he *was* God's Anointed One. Then how could God let Israel turn away?

St. Paul wrestled with the problem. His discussion forms the central part of his most important letter— *Romans.* His answer is four-fold. (1) What has happened

[5] Below, pages 233ff.

simply represents God's way of working out His purpose. Man has no right to question what God has done, any more than a lump of clay may question what the potter makes of it. (2) If Israel had accepted Messiah, the Gospel might never have been preached to Gentiles. Israel's failure made it providentially possible for non-Jews to learn about Christ. (3) Eventually Israel *will* accept Messiah, and 'be saved.' It is here that St. Paul breaks into the marvelous hymn,

O the depth of the riches both of the wisdom and the knowl-
    edge of God!
How unsearchable are his judgments, and his ways past
    tracing out!
For of him, and through him, and unto him, are all things.
To him be the glory for ever. (*Romans 11:33,36*)

(4) In the meantime there is this new branch, the Church, which has been engrafted into the trunk of Israel's life. From now on the full Christian Church shares in Israel's heritage. The Church is descended from Abraham, spiritually for the most part but no less actually and completely. That is, *the Church is the new Israel* in covenant with God as really and effectually as the old Israel had been. St. Paul thinks of the Church as in a most important sense replacing the ancient people, and thereafter playing the same role that Israel once had done.

God is unchangeable. He does not alter His way of working with mankind. If His chosen people fail, then by His very nature and method He must place His Covenant with a new people. Eight centuries before Paul, the prophet Amos had warned that that might happen.

Three expressions which recur constantly in the New Testament emphasize the fact that the Church is the new Israel, and is in covenant with God. The first is *the Body of Christ*. This figure is a favorite in the *Epistle to the*

Ephesians. Elsewhere, St. Paul develops it to show how the individual Christian is related to the whole Church. One ought not to demean himself, or his brother, because all of us are members of an organism, the Christian community. That organism depends for its life on the proper functioning of every part.

Just as surely, no member can function apart from the organism. A thoughtful person might work out, all by himself, a religion that is both beautiful and intellectually stimulating. He might even name the name of Jesus in it. Unless his faith leads him, however, not only to serve his fellowmen but to serve *with* them, and to worship with them in the name of Christ, it will not be Christianity.

Second, consider the figure of *the Bride and the Bridegroom.* In the Old Testament, as we saw, the prophets drew from the figure of marriage some of their greatest lessons about the binding relation between God and His people. Yet New Testament writers use an almost identical figure to portray the relation between Christ and his followers:[6]

John [the Baptist] answered and said, I am not the Christ, but I am sent before him. He that hath the bride is the bridegroom: but the friend of the bridegroom rejoiceth greatly because of the bridegroom's voice: this my joy therefore is made full.

Let us rejoice and be exceeding glad, and let us give the glory unto him: for the marriage of the Lamb is come, and his wife hath made herself ready.

The husband is the head of the wife, as Christ also is the head of the Church. Husbands, love your wives, even as

[6] Most of the following quotations are abridged. It would be well to read the entire passages in the New Testament:
John 3:22-30;
Revelation 19:6-10; see also 21:9-11; 22:17;
Ephesians 5:23-32.

Christ also loved the Church, and gave himself up for it: that he might present the Church to himself a glorious Church, holy and without blemish. Even so ought husbands to love their own wives as their own bodies, even as Christ also the Church; because we are members of his body.

This mystery is great; but I speak in regard of Christ and of the Church.

In the last passage it is hard to say whether the author's chief purpose was to compare Christianity to marriage, or to compare marriage to Christianity in its sacred and enduring nature. In either case the figure points to the nature of the Church. Like Israel of old, the Christian community is a single people in covenant with her Lord. So today, in words we all know, the Church continues to say that matrimony 'signifies unto us the mystical union that is betwixt Christ and his Church.'

Finally, New Testament writers use the word *covenant* itself. The term occurs some 33 times, about half of them being in the *Epistle to the Hebrews*. 'Our sufficiency is of God,' wrote St. Paul, 'who also made us ministers of a new covenant' (*II Corinthians 3:5-6*). The author of *Hebrews* quotes Jeremiah, 'Behold the days come, saith the Lord, that I will make a new covenant,' and then goes on to say,

In that he saith, a new covenant, he hath made the first old. But that which is becoming old and waxeth aged is nigh unto vanishing away. Now even the first covenant had ordinances of divine service. But Christ, who through the eternal Spirit offered himself without blemish unto God, is the mediator of a new covenant.

Ye are come unto mount Zion, the heavenly Jerusalem, and to Jesus the mediator of a new covenant.

Now the God of peace, who brought again from the dead the great shepherd of the sheep with the blood of an eternal covenant, even our Lord Jesus, make you perfect in every good thing to do his will, working in you that which is well-pleasing in his sight, through Jesus Christ; to whom be the glory for ever and ever. (*Hebrews 8-13 passim*)

Christians today, Roman Catholic, Greek Orthodox, Methodist, Presbyterian, Episcopalian, are accustomed to stand and say publicly, 'I believe in the holy catholic Church.' Some Protestants object to that, not understanding the adjectives. 'Catholic' does not mean 'Popish'; it means, literally, 'according to the whole' (Greek *kat' holon*). 'Holy' means 'set apart to God.' So, in his Creed, the Christian registers what is the mountainous import of the entire New Testament. God has, through His Christ, established this community in the world, this covenanted totality, this Christian people. For twenty centuries, now, it has been His arm in history.

CHAPTER VI

JESUS AND THE COVENANT

The Gospel of Luke says that Jesus was about thirty when there appeared, in the southern part of the country, a strange, wild figure. He was Jesus' cousin, Luke asserts; yet two men could hardly have seemed more different. Jesus was friendly and socially inclined, so much so that his opponents complained about his associates and called him a glutton.[1] John the Baptist drew no such complaints. He lived meagrely, his gaunt frame clothed in skins. He made the desert his home. He preached a frightening, fire-and-brimstone gospel.

At about the point where the Jordan River empties into the Dead Sea, John took his stand. The crowds, doubtless small at first, grew rapidly as the people flocked to listen to him, and to be baptized. He told them that danger was upon them for their sins, that God is no easy-going parent but a stern Judge who will shortly come to reward the good and punish the evil. They should take small comfort from the fact that they were the Chosen People, for *God could raise up a chosen people wherever He wished—* even out of these stones!

Jesus too came to John, and was baptized. Immediately thereafter the Spirit of God drove him—'drove' is the

[1] Jesus himself discussed the latter charge, Matthew 11:16-19; Luke 7:31-35. See also Mark 2:14-17.

word the Gospels use—into the wilderness. There, after six weeks of fasting, he faced temptation.[2] Since Jesus was alone, the story of his temptations can have come from no one but himself. They are described with the same brilliant imagery that marks so much else that he said.

Satan accosted him. 'If thou art the Son of God. . . .' In ancient times, 'son of God' had many meanings. Among pagans it might imply no more than 'hero' or 'great man.' In Jewish idiom the whole nation of Israel was sometimes called God's son. Now and then the phrase was applied to an angel or other superhuman being. Often it meant the Messiah, and that seems to have been its meaning here.[3]

Many Jews thought that Messiah would bring a 'feast of fat things, of wines on the lees.' They pictured a time when every vine should bear a thousand branches, every branch a thousand clusters of grapes; when the stomachs of Israel should be full and its enemies' stomachs empty. Jesus himself had gone without food for forty days when Satan said to him, 'If thou art the Son of God, command that these stones become bread.'

Others thought Messiah was to be a great king. Since the enemies of God's people are God's own enemies too, Messiah would trample Israel's foes under foot. He would set up a political government, with the capital at Jerusalem. Then the other nations would, as vassals, pay painful tribute to this people whom they had once abused. So persistent was this belief that it led, later, to a most poignant incident. After the disciples had been through the catastrophe of Jesus' arrest and death, and then the ineffable experience of his resurrection, they still could ask,

[2] Jesus' temptation is recounted at Matthew 4:1-11 and Luke 4:1-13. Mark has a much abbreviated account at 1:12-13.
[3] See below, pages 155f; 233.

'Lord, wilt thou at this time restore the kingdom to Israel?' In the wilderness now, Jesus was transported (in spirit, if not physically) to a high mountain. There he could see the vast panorama of the world spread out before him. Satan said to him, 'All this I will give thee, if thou wilt fall down and worship me. For it is all mine, and to whomsoever I will, I give it.'

Finally he was taken to the Holy City. Of all the popular ideas about Messiah, the most thrilling was that he should come suddenly from the skies to lead Israel to victory. What could more surely prove Jesus' claim, then, than to leap unhurt down into the midst of Jerusalem's throngs? 'If,' said Satan, 'thou art the Son of God, cast thyself down [from the pinnacle of the Temple]. For it is written, He shall give His angels charge concerning thee, and, On their hands they shall bear thee up lest thou dash thy foot against a stone.'

Fill his own and the people's bellies? Be a military and political conqueror? Come miraculously from the sky? To a Jew, and especially to a Galilean, these would have seemed an open road into Messiah's Kingdom. Jesus knew that they were not. 'Get thee behind me, Satan! It is written, Thou shalt worship the Lord thy God, and Him only shalt thou serve.'

He must summon Israel to reconstitute the ancient faith. Under the Covenant Israel had learned, as we saw, that God alone is sovereign. Now Jesus proclaimed the Kingdom of God, a dominion so awe-inspiring, so desirable that a man must surrender all he owns, even his arm or his eye, even his home, rather than lose it.

Israel had learned, also, that God wants man to be good. Now Jesus raised the moral demand to highest pitch. 'Ye shall be perfect, as your heavenly Father is perfect!' He did not pretend that his way was easy. 'Narrow is the gate, and straitened the way that leadeth unto life, and few are they that find it.' He insisted, however, that it was possible. 'Whosoever heareth these words of mine, and doeth them, shall be likened unto a man that built his house upon a rock.' [4]

In Israel's lore, marriage had depicted God's covenant with His chosen people. Jesus' parables abound in the figure.[5] They indicate that, with supreme audacity, he took the word which Israel had used of very God and turned it to himself: 'The Bridegroom came, and they that were ready went in with him to the marriage feast.' 'Can the children of the bridechamber fast while the Bridegroom is with them? The days will come when the Bridegroom shall be taken away from them, and then will they fast in those days.'

So he summoned Israel to himself. 'Ye have heard it said to them of old time . . . , but *I* say unto you . . .' 'Wheresoever two or three are gathered together in my name, there am I in the midst of them.' 'Whosoever confesseth me before men, him will I confess before my Father.' 'Come unto me, all ye that travail and are heavy laden, and I will refresh you.' [6]

At first he seems to have been successful. Mark says that Jesus' fame spread first through the surrounding area of Galilee, and then farther until it reached Jerusalem, four days' journey to the south. The common people heard him gladly. They came in increasing crowds—largely, no doubt, because he was able to heal disease. So intense was the stir, so powerful was his mien, that his friends kept asking themselves, 'Who is this man?' Strangers asked it

[4] These words are from the Sermon on the Mount, Matthew 5-7. It would be worth while to read the entire sermon at this point.
[5] See Matthew 22:1-12; 24:37-39; 25:1-12; Mark 2:19-20; Luke 12:35-38; 14:7-10.
[6] Matthew 5:21-47; 18:20; 10:32; 11:28-30.

too, and then offered various answers: 'A prophet.' 'Elijah come back to life.' 'John the Baptist come back to life'— for Herod had beheaded John in the meantime.[7]

Soon, however, there was opposition. It began among the Jewish leaders, spread to Herod's court and then, apparently, to the excitable but fickle multitudes. Jesus had claimed to forgive sins, which to the more pious Jews was sheer blasphemy. He preached with a new authority that was bound to arouse envy. Toward the Law of Moses he took a stand which, in both word and act, seemed to many to play fast and loose with sacred things.[8] Worst of all, to not a few, his healing ministry looked like witchcraft. 'By Beelzebul, the prince of demons, he casteth out demons.' (*Mark 3:22*) A hundred years later, the rabbis were still saying that Jesus had brought magic spells from Egypt and that he was executed for sorcery.

So the Pharisees and the Herodians—as it were, the religious leaders and the politicians—consulted together how to put a stop to Jesus' ministry. Some one told Jesus that Herod too was seeking his life. 'It cannot be,' Jesus replied, 'that a prophet perish outside Jerusalem.'

Even if one disbelieves the miracle stories in the Gospels, and doubts that Jesus was divine, still one must recognize two facts. First, Jesus was a Jew, steeped in the religion of the Old Testament. Second, like many of the ancient prophets, he was a statesman. Therefore, to understand what follows, we must once again look at the world as a first century Jew, a Jew of statesmanly vision, would have regarded it. For fourteen hundred years Israel had been the Chosen People, the beloved community, the

[7] This was Herod Antipas who, under Roman supervision, governed Galilee and some land east of the Jordan. Do not confuse him with Herod the Great, who reigned when Jesus was born but who died in 4 B.C.
[8] See below, Chapter XII.

arm of God and His voice in the world. Israel had longed for a Messiah. Then Messiah came. He called upon Israel to find again the righteousness of God, the sovereignty of God, the sacredness of suffering, the fulfilment of God's purpose in His Anointed One.

Israel was summoned. Israel refused. *What must the outcome be?*

To Jesus, loyal and fervent Jew, the answer was stark tragedy. *Israel was doomed.* Within a generation it would be destroyed. (It was in fact destroyed about forty years later.) The dark shadow of the Cross was made blacker still by his foreknowledge. He spoke of it again and again.[9]

Then began he to upbraid the cities wherein most of his mighty works were done, because they repented not. Woe unto thee, Chorazin! woe unto thee, Bethsaida! for if the mighty works had been done in Tyre and Sidon which were done in you, they would have repented long ago in sackcloth and ashes. But I say unto you, it shall be more tolerable for Tyre and Sidon in the day of judgment, than for you. And thou, Capernaum, shalt thou be exalted unto heaven? thou shalt go down unto Hades: for if the mighty works had been done in Sodom which were done in thee, it would have remained until this day.

He must leave Galilee. Actually he made two excursions, before his final journey to Jerusalem. The first was to the north-west, near the very Tyre and Sidon of which he had spoken. Just one incident is recorded on this trip, but it is very revealing. A Gentile woman came, seeking healing for her daughter who lay ill—'grievously tormented,' the mother said. The bitter disappointment of his people's rejection welled up in Jesus' reply. 'I was sent only to the lost sheep of the house of Israel!' 'True, sir,' the mother answered, 'but even the dogs eat the crumbs

[9] Matthew 11:20-24; Luke 10:13-16.

that fall from the master's table'—the Gentiles, too, may share in the Gospel. Jesus healed the little girl. Mark explicitly says he did it because of the Gentile woman's words.

The second excursion was to the area of Caesarea Philippi. (This was Caesarea in the region governed by Philip. Do not confuse it with Caesarea on the coast, where St. Paul was later imprisoned.) There Simon Peter made his great confession, 'Thou art the Messiah.' From there Jesus turned southward for the last time, his face set toward the Holy City. The sternness, which marked his reply to the Gentile mother, was evident again and again as he made his way.[10]

Toward the end of the journey Jesus and his friends came over the brow of a hill. Below them lay a tiny valley. Beyond was Jerusalem. It was Passover time. Every approach to the town was choked with travelers, urged on by the wish to celebrate the feast within the walls of the Holy City. At this sacred season every Jew remembered: Once before, at Passover, the Lord God had freed His people from their foreign masters. Would He do it again? Sometimes at Passover the people got excited, and rioted. So Pilate, the Roman governor, enlarged his police force. The disciples fetched a donkey. Jesus sat on it, and thus made his way into the city. Suddenly his people's bitter fate swept over him. 'O Jerusalem, Jerusalem! How oft would I have gathered you as a hen gathers her chicks under her wings, but ye would not. Behold, from henceforth your house is left unto you desolate.' [11]

The next day Jesus did a bizarre thing. He and his

[10] See below, pages 168f.
[11] Luke 19:41-44 places the lament over Jerusalem at this point, with another (Luke 13:34-35) somewhat earlier. Matthew 23:37-39 puts it a few days later. In each case it is Israel's rejection of Jesus, and the ensuing tragedy, that evoke the words.

group had taken lodging in Bethany, a few miles from Jerusalem. In the morning, walking back to the city, he saw a fig tree in the distance. He went up to it, looking for fruit—even though, Mark says, it was not the season for figs. When Jesus found no fruit, he drew back and cursed the tree!

More than any other incident in the New Testament, this one has troubled readers both clergy and lay. Did Jesus give way to angry petulance? Was he, perhaps, emotionally disturbed by the catastrophe that awaited him? The incident must have distressed St. Luke, for he left it out of his Gospel and inserted, instead, a parable about a fictional tree. Yet in its context, Jesus' act was entirely fitting. The Jews had expected that, when Messiah came, bizarre and unexplainable things would occur. By its very grotesqueness, Jesus' act announced his claim. Indeed a still closer link may be seen between the cursing of the tree and the events before and after it. The tree is a common symbol in Judaism and Christianity (as it is in other religions). It represents the tree of life, or it stands for the commitment of God to His people. Here, then, Jesus was acting out a parable. Like the tree, Israel was unready when Messiah came. 'If they do these things in the green tree,' he was to say later, 'what will they do in the dry?' Israel brought forth no fruits of repentance such as John the Baptist had sought. Now she disclaimed her destiny. 'Henceforth,' Jesus said, 'let no man eat fruit of thee for ever.' Immediately, says Matthew—the next day, says Mark—the tree withered up from its roots.

Arrived in the city again, Jesus became involved in debates with Jewish religious leaders. He told them a story.[12]

[12] Mark 12:1-12; Matthew 21:33-41. In Mark, at the end of the parable the owner will *give* the vineyard to other husbandmen, while in Matthew he will *let it out* to them. We have substituted a phrase that covers both meanings.

A man planted a vineyard, and set a hedge about it, and digged a pit for the winepress, and built a tower, and let it out to husbandmen, and went into another country. And at the season he sent to the husbandmen a servant, that he might receive from the husbandmen of the fruits of the vineyard. And they took him, and beat him, and sent him away empty. And again he sent unto them another servant; and him they wounded in the head and handled shamefully. And he sent another; and him they killed: and many others; beating some, and killing some. He had yet one, a beloved son: he sent him last unto them, saying, They will reverence my son. But those husbandmen said among themselves, This is the heir; come, let us kill him, and the inheritance shall be ours. And they took him, and killed him, and cast him forth out of the vineyard. What therefore will the lord of the vineyard do? He will come and destroy the husbandmen, and will turn the vineyard over to others.

Certainly these words predict Jesus' death. Likewise, however, they are a most solemn declaration about Israel. This chosen people had been given the vineyard of the Lord to till; but it had rejected the prophets, and now would condemn to death the Son whom God had sent. What then would the Lord God do? He would not change His *way* of working with men. He must put His vineyard into the keeping of another people, to till it and to bring forth fruits worthy of their great commission.

The Temple where Jesus spoke these words was the third in Israel's history. On their way out, Jesus' disciples remarked on the magnificent beauty of the nearly finished structure. Jesus answered, 'Do you see these buildings? I tell you, there will not be left of them one stone standing upon another.' The nation of Israel was about to cease to be. The Temple with the Holy of Holies would be destroyed, never to rise again. To the mind of a first century Jew that would be the most fearful cataclysm that man could dream.

Here the Christian confronts a solemn, awful question. The nation did, in fact, come to an end a scarce generation after Jesus spoke, and its Temple was obliterated. Then is there any truth, any truth at all, in Jesus' interpretation? Did some new people arise, with a new Holy of Holies, to take Israel's place? If this be true, or any part of it, there lies upon the Christian community a most portentous task. We are, as St. Paul declared, ourselves the new Israel. If God is King, the Christian community is His domain and the extension of His work in the world. Here is the truth in the old and much misunderstood saying, *Extra ecclesiam nulla salus,* 'Outside the Church there is no salvation.' This does not mean that to get to heaven one must join a particular group. It means that, to be fully Christian, one must *share* one's religion, with and through the community of the faithful. That is how God works.

To be fully Christian is to say and mean not 'I' but 'we.' '*Our* Father, who art in heaven . . . Thy kingdom come . . . Give *us* this day our daily bread. And forgive *us our* trespasses, as *we* forgive those who trespass against *us*. And lead *us* not into temptation, but deliver *us* from evil. For thine is the kingdom. . . .'

CHAPTER VII

CHRIST OUR PASSOVER

A few days later Jesus sent two disciples from Bethany into Jerusalem. He asked them to go to a particular house and there prepare a supper for himself and his companions. (Many believe that this was the house of John Mark, the author of one of our Gospels.)

There is considerable doubt as to whether Jesus' Last Supper was a Passover meal or not. The Gospel of John seems to say that it was not. The Jewish day began at sunset. According to the Gospel of John, the meal took place just after the sunset of the twenty-four hour period *preceding* the start of the feast. In that case Jesus never got to eat the Passover, but was slain just at the time the lambs were being slaughtered for the great day. St. Paul and some other early Christians may have thought this. For example St. Paul said, 'Christ our Passover is sacrificed for us' (*I Corinthians* 5:7). This would fit the belief that Jesus was killed at the same time as the sacrificial lambs.

Yet the first three Gospels are even more explicit that the Last Supper *was* a Passover meal; and that it was eaten just after the sunset when, by Jewish reckoning, the Passover festival had begun.

It has been suggested that astronomy could solve the problem. (a) Passover was set for the day of the full moon. (b) All the Gospels agree that Jesus died on a Friday. Why not, then, see whether the Passover full moon did fall on a Friday in any of the years around this time? If so, then the first three Gospels are probably right. If not, and if the Passover full moon fell on Saturday in any of those years, the Fourth Gospel is probably right. The trouble here is that we cannot be sure how accurate the Jews themselves were, at this period, in determining the phases of the moon. Without scientific training or proper instruments, they could be a day off in their calculations—especially if there were cloudy weather!

Others would solve the difficulty by reference to Jewish religious scruples. Within the twenty-four hour period of Jesus' death we find the disciples carrying swords. Joseph of Arimathea makes purchases. At Jesus' trial the Jewish leaders leave the business of the Temple, enter the court of the uncircumcised Romans, excite the people to go out of the city and make sport of the dying victims at the execution ground. Does all this seem fitting behavior for a sacred day? Many students think that it does not, and hence that the Gospel of John is right: Jesus was killed before the Passover had begun. Once more, however, the solution is less simple than it seems, because we lack information. Much more is known about Palestinian life in the first century B.C., and in the second century A.D., than for the time when Jesus lived. The reason is that Palestine was overrun and Jerusalem and its environs were destroyed in A.D. 70. With the destruction went the records of just those years we should like most to know about. Therefore we cannot really say which, if any, of the above activities would have been impossible on the great day of the feast.

A more dependable answer may come from examining

just what Jesus and his companions did at the Last Supper. (a) Jesus wished to eat the meal within the Holy City. (b) He asked his friends to prepare it with special care. (c) It was eaten after sunset. (d) Only Jesus' most intimate companions came with him. (e) The Fourth Gospel says that, when Judas left, the others thought he was going out to give alms (*John 13:29*). (f) Jesus broke the bread, took the cup and, when he had given thanks, explained their meaning. (g) He compared the wine to blood, which seems to mean that it was red wine. (h) The meal closed with a hymn. (i) The group did not go back to Bethany afterward, but stayed near Jerusalem.

Every one of these features was typical of Passover customs, both before and after Jesus' time. In contrast, none of them fits what we know of any other Jewish meal. Furthermore, while the Jewish leaders normally avoided court actions on the sacred day, they *would* try a 'false prophet' at such a time. Indeed that kind of trial could take place only at a feast, because the Law of Moses required that 'all Israel' be present.[1] The priests' wish to apprehend Jesus 'not on the feast' meant simply that the initial arrest was to be secret. The trial itself was public enough.

So, although the information is not quite conclusive, it seems probable that the Last Supper was a Passover meal. Even if it was not, however, the impending festival was in every one's mind. Therefore the following interpretation holds good.

The glimmering olive-oil lamps cast leaping shadows about the room. In the manner of the traditional Passover rite, Jesus broke bread and passed it. Then he passed a cup of wine and, again in the ancient custom, explained

[1] At least, that is how the rabbis interpreted Deuteronomy 13:1-11.

the meaning of this meal. If the custom was old, the words were new. They burned into the disciples' memories, never to be forgotten.

To understand what Jesus did, we must go back once more to the first Passover of all.[2] In that night, so Israel believed, God had redeemed His people from slavery. No Passover since then had been redemptive in the same way. They were all memorials, to commemorate that one great deliverance. In speaking of the Passover, Jews sometimes used the phrase, 'the body and the blood.' This referred always and only to the lambs killed for the celebration.

Jesus broke the bread and passed it. 'This is my body.' He blessed the cup and passed it. 'This is my blood.' Here, then, was a Passover indeed, but such a one as no man listening had ever dreamed. *It was the second redemptive Passover in all history.* As on that fateful night fourteen centuries before, God was once again intervening to set a people free. The slavery was a different slavery. The body and blood were a different body and blood. And the people was to be a different people.

'This is my blood—of the *new Covenant.*' In that supreme and focal sentence is summed up all that he had stood for, and all that he had done. It is the import of his ethical teaching. Christian morality is no mere adherence to a set of precepts. It stems from a pact, between God and a Christian people. It reflects the understanding of the ancient prophets, that God is righteous and asks man to be righteous; but it reaches higher than any prophet could grasp. Indeed, Jesus set a moral standard so high that man, measuring himself against it, must for ever know his own littleness and his need of forgiveness. Covenant thinking means thinking about *that.*

[2] Above, pages 33f.

There, too, is the key to Jesus' teaching about the Kingdom. To offer his blood of the Covenant was to reëstablish the engagement of God with man, and man's awareness of God's own sovereign power. It was to set into the world again a people through whom and to whom he could say, 'Lo, I am with you alway, even unto the end of the world.'

There, finally, is the meaning of Jesus' thought concerning himself. Like the prophets before him, he proposed that the fulfilment of the divine purpose must be through the Messiah and through the Suffering Servant of the Lord. The new and startling thing was that he brought these figures together, and made them the sum of his own claim.[3]

Much ink has been spilled over the question whether Jesus said, 'My blood of the Covenant' or 'of the *new* Covenant,' for both forms appear in various strands of the New Testament. Actually it makes little difference. In either case his words are the seal of a new or, at the least, a newly constituted order. They mark a new Passover, when God intervened in the night to deliver His people out of slavery and into His flaming light.

That is why St. Paul proclaimed, 'Christ our Passover is sacrificed for us.' It is why as Christians we sing at Communion, 'Holy, holy, holy, Lord God of hosts. Heaven and earth are full of thy glory: Glory be to thee, O Lord Most High.' In the body and blood of this *new Covenant*, the *new Israel* has found its Holy of Holies.

[3] We shall have more to say about each of these implications of Jesus' words. On his ethics, see below, pages 151f., 188f.; on the Kingdom, pages 158ff.; on his bringing together of Messiah and Suffering Servant, pages 167ff.

THE SECOND KEY:

THE NEW AGE

CHAPTER VIII

SOME LONG WORDS
AND THEIR MEANINGS

One feature of Covenant thinking may have struck you again and again, viz., its concern about the future. 'God is going to conquer evil,' thought the Israelite. 'He is going to set Israel free. He is going to send His Messiah.' Other religions, all the way from Greece to China, might suppose that the Golden Age was in the past. Israel knew that the Golden Age was still to come. (Christianity knows it too.) In the decades before Christ, interest in the future grew so intense, and took on such special forms, that we must devote special study to it.

Christian scholars sometimes use long words. It will help us now, if we borrow a few of these. The first and most important is *apocalypse*, plus related words like *apocalyptist*, *apocalypticism* and *apocalyptic*. The word comes from Greek, and means 'what is uncovered' or 're-vealed': specifically, what is revealed about the future. An apocalypse is a book or piece of writing that contains such revelations. In the Bible, *Daniel* and *Revelation* are apoc-alypses,[1] and there is apocalyptic material in *Mark 13, I Corinthians 15, I* and *II Thessalonians* and other por-

---

[1] Never call the last book of the New Testament 'Revelations.' It is singular, *Revelation*.

tions of the New Testament. Most apocalypses, however, never got into the Bible.

Two other terms are likely, for various reasons, to be confused with *apocalyptic,* and they had best be cleared up at once.

The first is *prophecy.* This is sometimes used carelessly for 'predicting,' but its real meaning is 'proclaiming' or 'preaching.' The main task of the Hebrew prophets was to insist on moral goodness, and to encourage Israel to be loyal to God. Sometimes, of course, they did foresee what would happen; but that was incidental. The primary meaning of 'prophecy' is not *fore*telling, it is *forth*telling.

The next is *apocrypha.* This word means 'things hidden away.' Specifically it refers to books that were kept out of the Bible. Parts of the Old Testament apocrypha are accepted by some Christian bodies but not by all: *Baruch, Tobit, I* and *II Maccabees,* and so on. No Church admits any of the New Testament apocrypha into its Bible.[2] Some apocryphal books do happen to be apocalyptic in content, but that again is quite incidental.

We saw, in Chapter IV, how Israel was conquered in succession by Assyria, Babylonia, Persia, Greece and Rome. Rome was the master in Jesus' day, but it was from Persia and Greece that apocalyptic got much of its character. From the Persians the Jews took over ideas of heaven with its hierarchy of angels, and hell with its Satan and demons. The Jews, of course, developed these concepts far beyond anything in Persian religion, but the debt is plain. In books written before the Persian period such notions hardly appear at all, whereas they are prominent ever afterward.

Then after the next great invasion, by the Greeks, the

[2] A convenient collection of the latter is M. R. James, *The Apocryphal New Testament* (Oxford, Clarendon, 1924).

Jews became convinced that the age of prophecy had ceased. It would not return again until the time of the Messiah. Yet to be without prophecy was to be without direct guidance from the oracles of God. In a way, therefore, apocalyptic developed as a kind of substitute for prophecy, although the two are very different in character.

Seven features, in fact, distinguish apocalyptic from other religious writing.

1. *It uses the language of visions and dreams.* It is full of dragons, seas of glass, moons turning to blood, tongues like swords, etc. More than any other feature, this is what makes apocalyptic difficult and forbidding to modern readers.

Often, such imagery was used just because it was fashionable. That seems to have been the case, for example, in the *Book of Ezekiel.* Frequently, however, the dream language served as a useful secret code in times when the faithful were resisting oppression. Thus when the author of *Revelation* spoke of 'Babylon' or 'the great harlot,' few outsiders would recognize that he was talking about the Roman government! The beast, in the passage quoted on page 4, probably meant the Emperor Nero. The latter had died but, many people believed, had come to life again in the person of the Emperor Domitian. So he 'was, and is not, and yet is.'

Chiefly, however, dream language was used because apocalyptic seers really did have dreams and visions, which they recounted for the benefit of their readers.

2. *An apocalypse usually (not always) claims to have come from some famous man of old.* One such book is called 'The Assumption of Moses,' another 'The Testament of the Twelve Patriarchs' (Jacob's sons), and so on. An example in the Bible is the *Book of Daniel.* This was

actually written in 168 B.C., to encourage the Jews to resist Antiochus Epiphanes.[3] It is ascribed, however, to a man living under Nebuchadrezzar, four hundred years earlier. This was not dishonest. There was no law of copyright. The important thing was to get the book read. The author believed he was writing in the spirit of the ancient hero, and he applied that hero's courage and understanding to the later day.

3. *Apocalyptic appears in a time of stress and anguish,* when 'men's hearts are fainting them for fear.' That is understandable to any one who recalls the first half of the twentieth century. Apocalyptic was enormously popular during the wars and depressions of that period. Under catastrophe, people always long for supernatural help. They welcome reassuring visions of God soon coming to set things right.

4. *It is angry and resentful,* because of the suffering that has been heaped upon the people of God. It has much to say, therefore, about divine justice. It predicts how vengeance will be taken on the enemies of God.

On the other hand, apocalyptic says little about love or mercy or forgiveness. That is its greatest shortcoming.

5. Apocalyptic, however, does teach a noble and much-needed lesson: *God is all-powerful, and can be trusted to conquer evil.* Thus on almost every page of *Daniel* one meets passages like this:

I blessed the Most High, and I praised and honored him that liveth for ever; for his dominion is an everlasting dominion, and his kingdom from generation to generation: and he doeth according to his will in the army of heaven, and among the inhabitants of the earth: and none can stay his hand, or say unto him, What doest thou? (*Daniel 4:3-4*)

[3] See above, page 45.

In Handel's *Messiah,* the Hallelujah Chorus is taken directly from the book of *Revelation:*

> Hallelujah! hallelujah!
> For the Lord God omnipotent reigneth.
> The kingdoms of the world are become
> The kingdom of our Lord, and of his Christ,
> And he shall reign for ever and ever,
> King of kings, and Lord of lords.
> Hallelujah!

Similar hymns run all through apocalyptic literature. They reflect, of course, an intensifying of that faith in the sovereignty of God that had typified Covenant thinking.

6. *Apocalyptic warns its readers to be watchful,* because God is about to fulfil His purpose; *or else to be faithful,* because God will bless those who are loyal to Him despite adversity. As a rule, watchfulness is the keynote of earlier writers, who are fresh and vigorous. Faithfulness is the theme of those who have borne up long under 'the burden and heat of the day.'

Nearly every one who has gone to Sunday School remembers the story of Shadrach, Meshach, Abednego and the fiery furnace. The three men refused to worship an image that the pagan king Nebuchadrezzar had set up. The king threatened to have them thrown into the furnace, and finally he did it. The high point of the story is not the miraculous release of these men. The supreme moment comes in their reply to the king, before they know whether God will save them or not:

It may be that our God whom we serve will deliver us out of thine hand, O king. *But if not,* be it known unto thee, O king, that we will not serve thy gods, nor worship the golden image which thou hast set up. (*Daniel 3:17-18*)

'Though he slay me, yet will I trust him'—that is the kind of faith that apocalyptic seeks.

7. *Finally, apocalyptic divides all of history into two ages.* The present age is hopeless. It is tobogganing into ever worse torment and evil, until its end comes. Interestingly enough, apocalyptists, no matter when they lived, have nearly always expected the end within their own lifetimes. (If they did not, perhaps they would be less interested in it.)

The new age will be ushered in by a cataclysm. The Lord or His Messiah will descend on the clouds. The catastrophe will bring deserved chastisement to the foes of God. It will bring blessing and peace to His chosen ones.

At this point Jewish apocalyptists separated into two groups. (a) Some thought the new age would completely replace the present one. There would be an entirely new heaven and earth. A 'new Jerusalem' would be the capital. The wicked would be destroyed, or cast into a bottomless pit, or suffer other appropriate tortures. (b) Others thought the new era would be established within this present world. The latter would not be replaced; it would be cleansed and purified. Israel was to be the leading nation, and her former conquerors were to become her vassals. Scholars call the first type 'transcendental' apocalypticism, the second 'political.' A better term for the second might be 'intrahistorical,' since it held that the new age would be within the present historical order. The choice of adjectives is not important. The distinction itself is very important.

We need just one more long word: *eschatology* (pronounced 'eskatólogy'). This too is from Greek, and means 'doctrine of the last things.' It is broader than *apocalyptic* and covers any teaching about the end of the age, or about God's coming reign. All apocalyptic is eschatological, but not all eschatology is apocalyptic. Eschatology is apocalyptic only if it has the dream language, and the predictions of catastrophe and revenge, that we have described. Some eschatology is more sober than that, as we shall see.

CHAPTER IX

THE NEW AGE

For almost a century Palestine had lain under the heel of Rome. Yet Palestine was, to every good Jew, the 'inheritance of the Lord,' beloved by the Lord as His own. Let the Roman government be ever so enlightened (as, for its time, it was enlightened), still the Jew must hate it. The Covenant of the Lord was not with Rome but with Israel. The Jew longed for release, and for the setting up of that Kingdom which, he fervently believed, was promised through the Covenant.

The Jews, at least male Jews, were highly literate in Jesus' day. Being so anxious for Israel's release, then, they turned avidly to the apocalyptic books that used to appear. In Jerusalem, it is true, the apocalyptic hope was less strong than in Galilee. In and near Jerusalem dwelt the Sadducees or members of the priestly party. These people had fairly comfortable relations with the Roman government, and they were to a large degree financially secure and content with their lot. So they grew cynical about a new age, and did not encourage speculation about it.

Galilee was far to the north, and cut off from those influences. Apocalypticism, and eschatology of all sorts, were rife in Galilee. Scores of apocalyptic books had been produced, and the Galilean peasants read them and eagerly talked them over. Here also, people nurtured their memories of the time, a hundred years ago, when their land had last been independent. The independence had been won, in 144 B.C., by the Maccabees.[1] Often a Galilean father would name his son for one of the Maccabean heroes, Judas, Simon or Jonathan. Several of Jesus' disciples bore those names.

While the apocalyptists waited for God to intervene, another group, called the *Zealots*, wanted to take matters into their own hands: raise a force, start a rebellion, and throw off the Roman yoke. At least one of Jesus' disciples was a Zealot. Different from each other as Zealots and apocalyptists were, both groups looked for the time when the Kingdom would be restored to Israel.

So it was natural, when the disciples came under Jesus' terrific impact, that they should wonder whether he was the one to lead their country to freedom. First they asked, 'Who is this man?' Then Peter said, 'Thou art the Messiah,' and Jesus accepted the designation. After that, Jesus tried agonizingly to show them what Messiahship meant, but they could not understand. They wanted a monarch, whose panoply differed from other kings' only in outshining them all. James and John came to him and requested that, when he assumed his reign, they might have the two thrones on either side of his. That made the other disciples angry—not because James and John were wrong about the future, but because they had tried to get ahead of their co-workers.[2] How unspeakably pathetic was the song the disciples sang as they trooped into Jerusalem:

Hosanna!
Blessed is he that cometh in the name of the Lord:

[1] You can read about it in I Maccabees, one of the books of the Old Testament Apocrypha mentioned in the last chapter.
[2] Mark 10:35-41. Matthew 20:20-21 says that James' and John's mother made the request on their behalf.

> Blessed is the kingdom that cometh,
> The kingdom of our father David:
> Hosanna in the highest! (*Mark 11:9-10*)

At the Last Supper, Jesus made a final effort to get them to comprehend. 'I say unto you, that this which is written must be fulfilled in me, And he was reckoned with transgressors: for that which concerneth me hath fulfilment.' 'Lord,' they replied, 'here are two swords.' [3]

In Gethsemane the Master was arrested, and most of the disciples jumped up and fled. Peter did follow along to the trial, but when accosted he denied that he had ever known Jesus. Before we condemn the perfidy of these men, let us see what had happened to them. They had dropped their jobs and everything that was dear to them, in the belief that Jesus was the One for whom Israel had waited. They had hazarded their lives and possessions in the hope that he, the Messiah, would abolish their servitude to Rome, reclaim the independence of his people, make them leaders of the world, and thus fulfil the divine promise. And Jesus had permitted them to do these things! When Peter said, 'Lo, we have left all and followed thee,' Jesus replied, 'There is no man that hath left house, or brethren, or sisters, or mother, or father, or children, or lands, for my sake, and for the gospel's sake, but he shall receive a hundredfold now in this time, houses, and brethren, and sisters, and mothers, and children, and lands . . . and in the world to come eternal life.' [4]

How he had let them down! Arrested as a common criminal, he could not protect himself, still less those who had given him so much. They too might be taken into

---

[3] Luke 22:37-38. The passage to which Jesus referred is Isaiah 53:12.
[4] Mark 10:29-30. Again it would pay to read the entire passage, Mark 10:17-31; also Matthew 19:16-30.

custody at any moment. Even if they escaped, their hopes and dreams lay shattered. Whatever this man Jesus might be, clearly he was not what they had thought. Of course they left him. Would not any one?

Thus came about the first great effect of Jesus' passion. His death, and supremely his resurrection, were a mighty catharsis which washed from these men's minds their narrow little suppositions. They had looked for a political master and warrior king. Now they could begin to see in Christ, not less than those things, but infinitely more. They examined their Scriptures again, and found meanings they had never dreamed of. So, they became convinced, the tragedy and triumph that they had witnessed were done 'by the determinate counsel and foreknowledge of God.' To Jesus the Messiah, they now said, 'All the prophets give witness' (*Acts 2:23; 10:43*).

With Jesus' death and resurrection began a whole series of startling events, all of which helped make the new faith possible. One day about six weeks after the Resurrection the Apostles were sitting together, perhaps in the same room where they had eaten the Last Supper.[5] Suddenly a great noise was heard and, the book of *Acts* says, tongues of flame seemed to come down on each of them. Enormously stirred, certain that this was the Spirit of God sweeping over them, they began to shout. They created so much disturbance that a crowd gathered. St. Peter went out and preached to the people. It was the first Christian sermon. It made three thousand converts.[6] Other moving experiences ensued, and other mass conversions.

[5] During Jesus' ministry these men were called *disciples* or 'learners.' After the Resurrection, when they were commissioned to proclaim the new faith, they were called *apostles,* i.e., 'those who are sent' or 'commissioned.'

[6] Acts 2:1-41.

· *81*

We must not suppose that, at this early date, the Apostles had worked out a systematic theology about the Father, the Son and the Holy Spirit. They were not ready for that, and they were much too busy. In fact, 'the Spirit of God,' 'the spirit of Christ,' and 'Christ in you' seem to have meant the same thing to them. (At least they did to St. Paul, and the other Apostles were less systematic thinkers than he.) What they knew in their souls was that this Spirit, by whatever name, was working in them and through them.

Take these astonishing events that kept happening. Add to them the apocalyptic faith of these men, and their deep belief in and respect for the Scriptures. The result was two great convictions.

First, *the new age has already dawned.* The Covenant promise has at last been fulfilled. Over and over in the New Testament the new era is described in the present or the past tense, as a phenomenon already begun:[7]

All authority *hath been given* unto me in heaven and on earth.
[Spoken by Jesus after the Resurrection.]

Those matters *have been fulfilled* among us.

God *hath made* him both Lord and Messiah, this Jesus whom ye crucified.

The gospel of God which he promised afore through his prophets in the holy Scriptures, concerning his Son . . . who *was declared* to be the Son of God with power, according to the spirit of holiness, by the Resurrection of the dead; even Jesus Christ our Lord, through whom we *received* grace . . . unto obedience to the faith among all nations.

[7] The following quotations, somewhat abridged, are from Matthew 28:18; Luke 1:1; Acts 2:36; Romans 1:1-7; Colossians 1:12-14; I Peter 1:10ff. and 2:9-10 respectively. To bring out the meaning more fully, we have occasionally departed from the ASV.

The Father . . . *delivered* us out of the power of darkness, and *transferred* us into the kingdom of his dear Son, in whom we *have* our redemption.

The prophets . . . prophesied of the grace that should come unto you. . . . To [them] it was revealed that not unto themselves, but unto you, did they minister these things, which *now have been* announced unto you.

Ye [Christians around the Mediterranean] are a chosen race . . . a holy nation, a people for God's own possession, that ye may show forth the excellencies of him who called you out of darkness into his marvellous light: who in time past were no people, but now are the people of God.

These quotations could be multiplied many times. They are one expression of an awareness that runs all through the New Testament. Something has happened. A new, exciting reality is now in the world. So important was this recognition that several modern scholars consider it the main stream in New Testament teaching about the future. *The future is already here!* [8]

Nevertheless, while the new era had begun, it certainly was not complete. In Jesus, the Christian certainly found *forgiveness* of sin, and perhaps he no longer *feared* death; but sin and death were themselves still painfully present. Most assuredly Jesus was the Messiah; but he was not yet reigning in that resplendent *visible* majesty that the prophets, and especially the apocalyptists, had described. So, in the second place, the Christians transferred to the future the, as yet unfulfilled, predictions of Hebrew-Jewish religion. Alongside the verses which speak of the new age as already here can be set at least as many that see it as still on its way and, apparently, coming soon:[9]

[8] Professor C. H. Dodd, who advocates this interpretation, calls the New Testament belief 'realized eschatology.'
[9] The following are from Romans 8:18-19; I Corinthians 7:29-31; Romans 13:11-12; Philippians 3:20; I Thessalonians 4:15ff.; II Peter 3:10-13; I John 3:2; I Peter 4:7 respectively.

The sufferings of this present time are not worthy to be compared with the glory which shall be revealed to us-ward. For the earnest expectation of the creation waiteth for the revealing . . .

. . . the time is shortened. . . . The fashion of this world passeth away.

Now is salvation nearer to us than when we first believed. The night is far spent, and the day is at hand.

Our citizenship is in heaven; whence also we wait for a Saviour, the Lord Jesus Christ.

We that are alive, that are left unto the coming of the Lord, shall in no wise precede them that are fallen asleep. For the Lord himself shall descend from heaven, with a shout, with the voice of the archangel, and with the trump of God. . . . But concerning the times and the seasons, brethren, ye have no need that aught be written unto you. For yourselves know perfectly that the day of the Lord so cometh as a thief in the night.

The day of the Lord will come as a thief; in the which the heavens shall pass away . . . and the earth and the works that are therein shall be burned up. . . . But, according to his promise, we look for new heavens and a new earth, wherein dwelleth righteousness.

It is not yet made manifest what we shall be. We know that . . . we shall be like him; for we shall see him even as he is.

The end of all things is at hand.

There are many passages like these. There are also longer sections, and one whole book, in which New Testament writers express an eschatological, yes, an apocalyptic faith. In one sense the new age may have begun; but in another, it is still to come. It will come soon. Its coming will be a cataclysm.

Does such a faith seem foreign to us, exotic and incredible? Well, our first task is not to please ourselves but to find out, as objectively as we can, what these early Christians really believed. Only then can we try to relate ourselves to their faith. On the other hand, as will be suggested in the next chapter, there is more truth to their apocalypticism than may at first appear.[10]

In the meantime notice two points. First, eschatology plainly is not the whole story about the New Testament. Most of the above passages are buried in contexts where the authors are talking chiefly about other things. Sometimes their subject is life after death; and they do not clearly separate this, in their minds, from the final end of the world. More often they are discussing the Christian way of life—morality, and fellowship under Christ our Head. They remind their readers that there will be a divine judgment upon human evil. The authors believe in the triumph of God. They hope it will be soon. This hope and faith are set, however, within the wide context of the whole Christian experience.

Second, notice *when and where the most intense New Testament apocalyptic appeared. Mark* 13 was published, probably, in Italy about the time of the Neronian persecutions. A generation later a more broadside persecution broke upon Christianity, under the Emperor Domitian, and it was then that *Revelation* and our Gospel of Matthew were composed.[11] *II Peter* is contemporary with a rebellion that broke out in Palestine in A.D. 132. In contrast, books like *Romans, Luke* and *Acts,* which contain very little apocalyptic, were produced in periods of comparative quiet. All this is just what we should expect. The

[10] See below, pages 93-95.
[11] That is, Matthew as we have it in the New Testament. An earlier form of the Gospel may have appeared in Palestine about A.D. 55. See Pierson Parker, *The Gospel Before Mark,* University of Chicago Press, 1953.

sharpest expressions of New Testament eschatology came when Christian people were frightened. Then they revived their apocalyptic hope, and they reminded themselves of every reassuring word that Jesus himself might have spoken about the future.

This brings us to the most serious question of all. What did Jesus think about the future? Did he share his followers' belief in a supernatural, divine intervention? If he did (and if he was wrong!), what kind of leader can he be for us today?

CHAPTER X

JESUS AND THE FUTURE

Today many people think of Jesus as the meek and gentle Christ, who taught his hearers to love God and one another, and to forgive their enemies; who himself 'when he was reviled, reviled not again; when he suffered, threatened not.'[1] However, that is but one side of the New Testament picture. There is another side, and it is much less comfortable.

When word came that John the Baptist had been thrown into prison, Jesus returned to Galilee and began his ministry there. At first, the Gospel of Matthew says, his preaching was identical with the Baptist's: 'Repent, for the Kingdom of Heaven is about to break in.' Thereafter, and all through his ministry, Jesus had a great deal to say about the coming judgment. Often he used the familiar figure of *Gehenna,* a valley outside Jerusalem where rubbish was burned. 'If thine eye causeth thee to stumble, pluck it out and cast it from thee: it is profitable for thee to enter into life with one eye, rather than having two eyes to be cast into the Gehenna of fire.' Frequently he spoke of the 'outer darkness': 'Then the king said, Bind [the offender] hand and foot and cast

[1] I Peter 2:23.

him into the outer darkness. There shall be the weeping and gnashing of teeth.' [2]

In many other ways Jesus spoke of an approaching divine judgment. He spoke also of his own position as Judge. Early in his ministry he declared, 'Many will say unto me in that Day, Lord, Lord . . . And I will say unto them. . . .' Shortly before his death he proclaimed the same thing: 'When the son of man shall come in his glory, he shall sit on the throne of his glory. And before him shall be gathered all the nations. And he shall separate them, as one divideth the sheep from the goats.' Between these two sayings were many others of the same tenor. 'When the son of man cometh, will he find faith on the earth?' 'Ye shall not have gone through the cities of Israel, till the son of man be come.' Even the Gospel of John, which seems less concerned than the others about the future, quotes Jesus as saying, 'He that believeth . . . I will raise him up at the last day.' 'I go to prepare a place for you . . . I will come again, and receive you unto myself, that where I am, there ye may be also.' At the trial before the Jewish authorities, the high priest demanded of Jesus, 'I adjure thee by the living God'—no devout Jew would refuse to answer that solemn charge—'I adjure thee by the living God: art thou the Messiah?' 'I am,' Jesus said, 'and henceforth ye shall see the son of man coming on the clouds of heaven.' [3]

Once he said, 'This generation shall not pass away, till all these things be accomplished.' 'Ye can foretell the weather. Can ye not discern the signs of the times?' [4]

Besides predictions like these, the Gospels say, Jesus foretold the immediate fates of himself and his followers.

[2] See Matthew 3:2; 4:17; 5:29-30; 8:12; 22:13; 25:30.
[3] See Matthew 7:22-23; 25:31-46; Luke 18:7-8; Matthew 10:23; John 6:37-54; 14:2-3; Matthew 27:63-64; Mark 14:61-62.
[4] Mark 13:30 (but read the whole of Mark 13); Matthew 16:1-4.

'Ye shall be hated of all men for my sake.' 'They shall drag you before kings and governors for my name's sake.' 'The cup that I drink shall ye drink also.' [5] 'The son of man is betrayed into the hands of sinners.' 'The son of man shall be taken, and mistreated and spit upon, and scourged, and slain. And after three days he shall rise again.' [6] The last prediction appears over and over again in the Gospel records.

He made more general predictions also. 'Pray to thy Father in secret, and thy Father that seeth in secret shall reward thee.' The importunate petitioner, he pointed out, will get the ear of the judge. 'Blessed are they that mourn, for they shall be comforted. Blessed are the peacemakers, for they shall be called children of God. Blessed are they that hunger and thirst after righteousness, for they shall be filled.' [7] All of the Beatitudes are of this sort. Taken by themselves such sayings might look like mere declarations, in pictorial language, that virtue will be rewarded. But they should not be taken by themselves. One of the most insistent features of apocalyptic thinking was its concern for the poor and needy, the oppressed and the dispossessed, and its determination that these be requited in the next age. In the light of Jesus' other words, therefore, this last group of sayings probably conveys his genuine expectation about the age to come.

Remember also certain features of Jesus' ministry that we glimpsed in earlier pages: When Peter called him Messiah, he accepted it. While he tried to dispel misconceptions from his friends' minds, nevertheless his own thoughts, like theirs, looked toward the future. He told

[5] Mark 13:9-13; 10:38-39.
[6] Mark 14:18-21,41-42; 8:31; 9:31; 10:33-34. In Palestine, as in other Oriental countries, lapse of time was reckoned inclusively. Friday afternoon, Saturday, and Sunday morning would count as three days.
[7] Matthew 6:2-6; Luke 18:2-7; Matthew 5:3-12.

them that they, who had given up much when they joined his movement, would be more than recompensed. On entering Jerusalem he let his followers fetch the donkey, throw their garments and branches from the trees onto the road before him, and sing of the approaching Kingdom.

The pattern runs through his ministry from beginning to end. Jesus was concerned for the future, for the end of the present age, perhaps even for the end of the world. Many New Testament students have thought that this preoccupation, this eschatology, was in fact Jesus' chief or only message. Some have gone so far as to say that he expected a final, supernatural world catastrophe within his own lifetime.[8]

If he did, he was mistaken. This thought alarms many people. It ought not to alarm. Whatever else we make of him, Jesus was thoroughly and completely human. As a man he might easily (some would say, *must certainly*) have been subject not just to physical limitations but to intellectual ones too. Jesus himself said, 'Of that day or hour knoweth no man, nor the angels in Heaven, *nor the Son;* but the Father only.' He was found in fashion as a man, and being as a man, he humbled himself.

That he might have been wrong ought not to distress us. Nevertheless, before we decide that he was in error we ought to notice some further facts about his teaching. First, as with the whole New Testament so with Jesus, eschatology was but a part, perhaps a very small part, of what he had to say. True, *Matthew* and *Mark* give a good deal of eschatology, though even they contain much besides. However, *Matthew* and *Mark* were produced, as

[8] For example, Albert Schweitzer in *The Quest of the Historical Jesus.* The first English edition of Schweitzer's book appeared in 1910 (German, 1906) and it has been of enormous influence ever since.

we saw, at times of persecution when the authors would be most apt to stress the apocalyptic element in Christ's words. How small a fraction of Jesus' life each author recorded can be seen from a little calculation. Jesus was perhaps thirty-three when he died, perhaps older.[9] Yet all that *Mark* tells about him could be compressed into ten weeks! *Matthew*, like *Luke* and *John*, covers a little more ground but not much. Every Gospel writer selected from the materials at his disposal; and in so doing he was guided by his own controlling interests in writing. Probably, therefore, we need to correct *Matthew* and *Mark* by *Luke's* and *John's* more balanced choice. In the last two, predictions of the future are not lacking but they are set in a vastly wider context.

Second, Jesus used to speak in parables. That is, he took familiar ideas and pictures from the life around him, and used them to teach moral and religious lessons. Regardless of his own literal beliefs, it would have been natural for him to use the apocalyptic imagery that was familiar to the Galileans, to convey his message. Now many of his sayings about the future occur in contexts where his chief emphasis plainly was not eschatology, but morality and faith. (That is true of a number of the sayings quoted above.) Here, at least, Jesus' apocalyptic language may have been intended not literally, but figuratively.

Third, and most important of all, Jesus was facing the destruction of Israel.[10] That may well have been what he

[9] There is no certainty about Jesus' age. The traditional 33 years are based on Luke 3:23 ('about thirty') plus some evidence for a three-year ministry. But Luke's words are by no means clear.

In John 8:57 it is said that Jesus was 'not yet fifty.' John 2:13-22 contains an elaborate cross-identification between Jesus and the Temple, which at that time had been 46 years in construction. This has led many, from the earliest times, to conclude that Jesus was the same age as the Temple, i.e., 46 when his ministry began.

[10] See above, pages 58; 61f.

meant when he said, 'This generation shall not pass away till all these things be accomplished.' [11] Can we feel, now, the anguish, the awful sense of doom, that Israel's coming ruin brought? This people, for twice seven centuries God's own arm in the world—this Temple, where the unchanging God Himself had chosen to dwell—these must cease to be. If ever the extreme language of apocalyptic was fitting, it fitted here. The fate of Israel meant the end of the age. It was like stars falling from their places, and moons turning to blood.

The death of Israel is almost enough, by itself, to account for every apocalyptic word that Jesus spoke. Almost, but not quite. Besides the end of his nation, Jesus did also foresee the end of this world, of this history.

When Jesus said of the Temple, 'There shall not be left one stone standing upon another,' it was one more violent blow to his eager but uncomprehending disciples. Presently they were outside the city and climbing the Mount of Olives. There they asked him, 'Master, when shall these things be?' 'Take heed,' Jesus replied. 'Let no one lead you astray.' With that he launched into what is known as the 'Apocalyptic Discourse.' It is probably second in fame only to the Sermon on the Mount. It is recorded in *Mark* 13, *Matthew* 24-26, *Luke* 21.

For at least two reasons, the Apocalyptic Discourse is often confusing to modern readers. For one thing, the Gospel authors could not always arrange their material in its original sequence, since they got it largely from Christian sermons, bits of oral tradition, and short written documents that had to be weaved together. Hence parts of this discourse may be out of place.[12] Indeed, parts of it may not even be Jesus' own, but a later expansion or

[11] Mark 13:30.
[12] Compare above, pages 5; 12.

paraphrase. In times of persecution, and without steno-
graphic reports of what he had said, such expansion
would be entirely natural.

On the other hand, Jesus himself was looking forward
to *two* great events: the smaller mountain of the destruction of Israel; then beyond it, but in the same perspective
of history, the huge mountain of God's final judgment and
sovereign coming for all the world.

It may be that Jesus did expect the end of the world
too soon; but that is hard to prove because, as we have
seen, often he was actually talking about the fate of
Israel, or about the fortunes of his followers. In contrast,
he apparently meant the final consummation of all things
when he said, 'Of that day or hour knoweth no man.' Yet
if the date was unsure, the fact itself was very sure. Most
of Jesus' later parables warned his followers to be on the
alert, ready constantly for the coming of the Lord. 'In an
hour when ye think not, the son of man cometh.' 'Watch,
for ye know not the day nor the hour.' 'Watch ye, lest
coming suddenly he find you sleeping.' [13] The old Israel
had not been ready. The new must be.

So again the solemn question comes: *Is there any truth
in Jesus' words?* For two thousand years the Church has
answered Yes. From time to time, it is true, individuals
or groups have appeared who took *Mark* 13, and *Revelation* and *Daniel*, crassly, and tried to set a date. Yet Jesus
himself warned against that, and most Christians have
heeded him. Not the date of the End but the *truth* of it
is what counts:

1. *God is really Sovereign.* What would it do to the
man of today if he really believed that? if it were the
unconscious assumption behind everything he did and
said? How would it affect even our reading of the daily

[13] Mark 13:32; Matthew 24:44; 25:13; Mark 13:35-36.

paper, if we *knew* that not all the machinations and stupidities of men and nations but only God is finally in control of the world? that His, and not ours, is the ultimate decision? that the perplexities of this or any other evil time are as dust in the balance beside His almightiness? Can we see it, this high mountain of the power of God, toward which Jesus gazed so long ago?

2. *We are accountable to God, and the accounting might come at any time.* Those are not comfortable thoughts. Nor are they the whole of the Christian gospel. Yet if we are honest with ourselves, most of us will recognize their truth. I *am* responsible for what I do; and I do not know when an accounting may come. I ought to live as though it might come at any moment. True, God is not only a Judge but also a loving Father, who stands ready to forgive. But to get His forgiveness, I must want it! I can ignore it, ignore Him, and even say a final 'No' to Him, for He has given me freedom to do these things. God will not force me, against my choice, to accept His forgiveness.

3. *The world,* that is, the course of history as we know it, *is moving toward a conclusion.* Is this a difficult concept? Then think what the alternative would mean. If there is no conclusion then there is no outcome, no final tying together of things or events. Then nothing is *really* at stake, in anything we do. What is not done today can be done tomorrow, or the day after that, world without end. Does not such a lack of consequence deny every instinct, every urge toward achievement, in the heart of mankind? The alternative to apocalyptic religion cannot be true.

Therefore apocalyptic religion, in its essential teaching, must be true. It is, once more, not the whole truth but a part of it. For our day it is a desperately needed part.

More than most of his ancestors, the twentieth century man needs to learn again that God is omnipotent; that man's striving has meaning; that, in the end, nothing but goodness will succeed.

That is why the Christian stands, week after week, century after century, with other Christians and declares, 'I believe in one God the Father Almighty, Maker of heaven and earth, And of all things visible and invisible: And in one Lord Jesus Christ . . . And he shall come again, with glory, to judge both the living and the dead; Whose kingdom shall have no end.'

THE THIRD KEY:

THE LAW

CHAPTER XI

THE PEOPLE OF THE BOOK

In the Palestine of Jesus' day a widening gap separated the common people from their religious leaders. The common people could not bridge this gap. Their leaders would not.

Many of the people belonged, as we have seen, either to the party of the Apocalyptists or to that of the Zealots.[1] Their religious leaders adhered chiefly, however, to two other parties, the Sadducees and the Pharisees. The Sadducees were the priestly party, from whose ranks came most of the service of the Temple. They lived largely in and near Jerusalem, where the Temple stood abuilding.[2] They were conservative. Origen, one of the great scholars of the early Church, said that the Sadducees accepted only the first five books of the Bible, regarding the rest as unscriptural. Origen may have been wrong about that, but certainly the Sadducees rejected much that other Jews had come to believe. For example, they denied the resurrection and life beyond the grave. Many of them were cynical over any Messianic hope—though they would not have declared their cynicism publicly. Also,

[1] Above, pages 72-73.
[2] This was the third and last Temple in Jerusalem's long history. It was begun under Herod the Great in 20 B.C. Two others, the Temple of Solomon and the Temple of Zerubbabel, had preceded it. The first was destroyed. The second had been heavily damaged by Herod himself.

they were worldly. Temple business was lucrative, and they were disposed to let well enough alone. They did not like to see agitation against their Roman overlords. They preferred to play along with the Roman authorities and keep in favor with them. Worldly, cynical, in league with Rome, rejecting the broader faith of the rabbis, and unconcerned for the common lot, they could give the people no inspired guidance.

The Pharisees were the party of the rabbis: doctors and teachers of the Scriptures, and expounders and preachers for the synagogues. Some people are surprised to learn that Jesus himself was in closer sympathy with the Pharisees than with any other religious group of the time. Like them he accepted the Prophets, as well as the Law, as authoritative Scripture. Like them, he believed in the resurrection. Like them, he moved about the land and taught in the synagogues. Indeed he once said of them, 'The Pharisees sit in Moses' seat,' that is, they rightfully expound the Scriptures. 'All things, therefore, whatsoever they command you, these do and observe.' [3] *The Acts* records that Pharisees joined the early Christian movement in considerable numbers. Saul of Tarsus, who became St. Paul, was one of them.[4] Yet, despite their fine qualities, the Pharisees have gained a reputation so evil that the very word 'Pharisaic' is a term of abuse! To understand the strength and weakness of these people, we must again dig back into history. We must see first of all how the ideas of *Law* and *synagogue* came into being.

In 621 B.C. there occurred what is known as the Deuteronomic Reform. For the first time Israel then received a written constitution. It was virtually the same as our present book *Deuteronomy*. It was composed by a group

---

[3] Matthew 23:2-3.
[4] See Acts 15:4-6; 23:6-8; 26:4-6.

of prophets and priests, who then 'hid' it in the Temple, in a spot where it was sure to be found. It was found, and taken to King Josiah. He was so impressed that he forthwith promulgated the book as the law of the land. Now Israel did not distinguish human from divine law, and both Josiah and the people accepted this as the written Word of God.

It is one of the ironies of history that this book, which was a joint enterprise of priest and prophet, in the long run undermined them both. Before *Deuteronomy*, the will of God had normally been made known through prophets consulting their oracles. After the reform, the increasing disposition of Israel was to consult not the voices of the prophets but this written and unchanging Word of the Lord. The prophets did not leave the scene at once. They gradually died out. By the time of the Greeks, it was easy for Israel to conclude that the age of prophecy had closed.[5]

The effect on priestly religion was more complex. In 586 B.C., scarcely thirty-five years after Josiah's reform, Babylonia conquered Palestine. Many Jews, and most of the Jewish leaders, were carried off into exile. There they remained for two generations. This was the great turning point in Israel's history, and scholars today divide everything in the Old Testament into 'pre-exilic' and 'post-exilic.' Coming on the heels of *Deuteronomy*, the Exile led to three major shifts in Israel's religion. While the changes took centuries to complete, they were all rooted in the deportation to Babylon.

1. Cut off from worship at the Temple, interest shifted to the written Word of God, and to its study and teaching. Around *Deuteronomy* as a nucleus, other written traditions from Israel's past were collected. Then a later

[5] See above, pages 72-73.

book, representing the priestly point of view, was added. The whole was woven together into what is now the first five books of our Bible. About 400 B.C., back in Palestine once more, this material was promulgated as *The Law*. It is commonly called the Law of Moses. While Moses could have written very little of it as it now stands, still it is appropriate to attach his name to it, for he had been Israel's founder and first lawgiver.

Thus there came about a change in emphasis that was both huge and permanent. Israel became the *am ha-Sefer*, the 'people of the Book.' Even today Jewish people call themselves that.

2. A new kind of worship became necessary, with a new center. These were found in the synagogue. The word 'synagogue' means a gathering together, for reading and expounding the Word of the Lord. The modern church service, such as Morning or Evening Prayer, is descended from the synagogue service. As this was eventually worked out, there were the congregation seated below, and the leaders before them on a rostrum. The congregation would join in chanting psalms, and in saying Israel's great confession of faith, 'Hear, O Israel, the Lord our God is one Lord.' [6] There would be reading from the Law, and from the Prophets. Then came an exposition of the text that had been read, somewhat on the order of the modern sermon. Outside the regular Sabbath services there was a school where boys learned to read the Hebrew Scriptures. The whole was supervised by the 'ruler of the synagogue,' a figure whom we meet sometimes in the Gospels. With all its similarity to modern services, synagogue procedure differed at one important point. The speaker who expounded the lesson might be chosen quite informally, and even after the service had

[6] Deuteronomy 6:4.

begun. The Gospels say that Jesus was often called upon in this way.

When Babylonia went down before Persia and the Persian king Cyrus allowed the Jews to return to Palestine, many of them settled not around Jerusalem but in Galilee to the north. After Persia came Greece, and then Rome; and under these the Jews began to move out into the Mediterranean world, making their homes in Egypt to the south, in Asia Minor, Greece and Italy to the north-west, and as far away as Spain. In these migrations they were again cut off from Jerusalem, but they could and did establish synagogues wherever they went.[7] In Jesus' day more Jews lived outside Palestine than in it, and synagogues were known everywhere.

During all this time the Temple at Jerusalem kept a powerful sentimental hold on Jewish minds. For ordinary life, however, the synagogue, not the Temple, was what counted. When the Temple was finally destroyed in A.D. 70, while it grieved the Jews deeply, it made scarcely a ripple in their every-day practice of religion.

3. Having the Law, and the synagogue in which to study it, Israel then had to have the teacher who should explain the Word of God; and the *scribe* whose duty was to copy it, and to copy the increasing mass of commentaries upon it. Often, teacher and scribe would be the same person. The conviction grew that this Law, this Word of the Eternal God, is inviolate. Every 'jot and tittle' of it is sacred and never to be changed. Each copy of the Law, then, must be exactly like every other. But there was no printing! Records were kept, showing the number of words and letters in each book of the Law, what word and what letter were at the exact center, and

[7] There was one attempt to found a Jewish temple in Egypt, but it was short-lived.

so on and on. Then each laboriously hand-written copy could be compared with the standard, and identity was secured.

This reverence for the letter was bound to affect beliefs about right and wrong, and even beliefs about God. What is right is right because the Law demands it. What is wrong is wrong because the Law forbids it. There is no appeal to a higher principle than that. So final, so absolute did the Law become that when the rabbis asked themselves, 'How does God pass His time?' their answer was, 'He reads the Law.'

In the time of Jesus, as we have seen, most teachers and scribes came from the ranks of the Pharisees. It is not certain just when or how the Pharisees got started. Apparently they began as religious liberals, who sought to give fresh interpretations to the Law so as to adapt it to the needs of a newer day. For generations, now, they had been at it. As so often happens, what had once been liberalism had now become orthodoxy, and even obscurantism. The Law, as the Pharisee interpreted it, must be obeyed. If for just one day, he thought, all Israel would obey the Law, then Messiah would come. So, over and over, he drummed obedience into his hearers' ears. He tried, himself, to obey. He was convinced in his soul that strict obedience was the will of God and the only hope for Israel.

If all Israel would obey! It was a large order, and the Pharisee knew it. He counted the commandments in the Law and found not ten, but six hundred and thirteen. He was right, as any one can verify for himself: there are just 613 injunctions in the first five books of the Bible. Yet great as that number is, it was but the beginning of the problem. Not all the commandments are explicit. It was man's duty, then, to discover how each ordinance was to be applied to daily living. So to each commandment of the Law the Pharisees had added interpretations—often voluminous interpretations—and these must be obeyed too. Take for example the commandment, 'Remember the Sabbath day, to keep it holy.' [8] Certainly that forbids work on the Sabbath—but what is work? How far may one walk before it becomes work? They settled on a 'Sabbath day's journey' of about half a mile. How many letters may one write? They decided that one letter would not be work, but two would be. Sewing one stitch is not work; two stitches are. A knot that can be tied with one hand is not work (do you agree?), but if it needs two hands, it is forbidden on the Sabbath. Of course, one must not cook on the Sabbath, though under certain restrictions one might keep food warm. Then what of an egg that was laid on the Sabbath? Here there were two schools of thought. The more conservative Pharisees, under Rabbi Shammai, said that the egg must not be eaten. Liberals, under Hillel, thought it could be.

Now watch an all too familiar scene. It is laid in a village street, one so narrow that you could stand in the middle and touch the walls on either side. Along the street a Pharisee is walking. Along the same street, from the opposite direction, comes a donkey driver with his beast. The two men see each other. The Pharisee knows, from long experience, that the donkey driver probably has touched something unclean, or has done more for his donkey on the Sabbath than the Law permits, thus disobeying the holy ordinance of the God of Israel. The donkey driver knows it too. All his life he has heard from the Pharisee how one ought to obey the Law, as the

[8] Exodus 20:8. Besides Exodus 20, there are sets of 'ten commandments' at Exodus 34, Leviticus 19 and Deuteronomy 5. All contain injunctions about the Sabbath. On the whole, the commandments in Exodus 34 and Leviticus 19 are more ritualistic than the other sets.

Pharisee understands the Law. The donkey driver believes, for he has been taught, that that is the only way he and his people can win the favor of God. He would like to obey—but how can you obey all those minute prescriptions, and still take care of a donkey? How can his wife obey, and still attend to the children and the thousand details of their home? Besides, uneducated man that he is, he just cannot remember all these explanations that the Pharisees keep giving out. He would like to obey. He knows he should. He cannot. He knows what will happen now. The Pharisee draws closer. The Pharisee is convinced to the core of his being that the donkey driver has sinned; and he knows that he, the Pharisee, must not touch the unclean thing. So, as they pass, the Pharisee draws in his skirts to avoid contamination from this disobedient son of Abraham.

Multiply that Pharisee by the scores, the hundreds who shared his deep conviction. Multiply the donkey driver by the thousands upon thousands of donkey drivers, farmers, potters, fishermen, tent-makers, and their wives and children. Small wonder that Jesus called the Pharisees 'blind guides, who bind men with burdens too heavy to be borne.' Small wonder that there came from his lips the cry, 'I have compassion upon the multitudes, for they are as sheep not having a shepherd.' Small wonder, finally, that he took a completely fresh attitude toward the Law, until it was said of him that 'he taught as one having authority, and not as their scribes.' [9]

[9] Matthew 23:4,16-20; Mark 6:34; Matthew 9:36; Mark 1:22.

CHAPTER XII

NOT AS THEIR SCRIBES

Jesus was a loyal Jew. He was thoroughly grounded in the Law and lore of Israel. Probably he learned to read in the synagogue school where he would study the Torah (i.e., the Law of Moses) and hear it explained. Luke says that Joseph and Mary went to the Passover celebration at Jerusalem every year, and that they taught the boy Jesus to do the same.

Later, his reverence for the Law was evident many times. One Sabbath day he and his disciples were strolling through a grainfield. The disciples began to pick and eat some of the grain, first rubbing it in their hands. Some Pharisees were watching, and they complained that the disciples were working—threshing grain!—on the Sabbath. Although Jesus came to his friends' defense, notice that he himself had plucked no grain. On another occasion, the Gospel of John tells how Jesus and his group were traveling through Samaria. This was a quasi-foreign area, sandwiched between the Jewish lands of Judea to the south and Galilee to the north. The disciples went into a Samarian village to buy food, something a strict Jew would have hesitated to do. Jesus did not go with them, and when they brought the food he did not eat it. Again, the Law of Moses required that when a person was healed of leprosy he must have a ceremonial cleans-ing as well. So when Jesus healed a leper, he insisted that the man go through the requirements of the ceremonial law.[1]

Incidents like these imply that Jesus was devoted to the Law. The same implication is seen in much that he said. Often he asked, 'Have ye not read in the Torah?' 'Is it not written in your Torah?' [2] Sometimes in dealing with the Scriptures Jesus sounded remarkably like the rabbis of his time, though his words had a pointed brilliancy which other teachers seemed to lack.[3] He was even interested, like the rabbis, in discussing which of the 613 commandments is the greatest. So it need not surprise us that many of his contemporaries called him 'rabbi' too. 'Till heaven and earth pass away,' Jesus declared, 'one jot or one tittle shall in no wise pass away from the Law, till all things be accomplished. Whosoever therefore shall break one of the least of these commandments, and shall teach men so, shall be called least in the kingdom of heaven: but whosoever shall do and teach them, he shall be called great in the kingdom.' [4]

Despite all this, the Pharisees not only called Jesus a sorcerer but charge that he played fast and loose with the Law! There could hardly have been a more serious indictment. To the Jewish mind the Law held a pillar position, second only to the Covenant itself. Israel was the People of the Book. That Book was no mere collection of statutes. It was the constitution, the backbone of Israel's structure, without which Israel could not exist. To

[1] Matthew 12:1-8; John 4:4-9,27-34; Mark 1:40-44.
[2] Matthew 12:5; Luke 10:26. The emphasis is constant in the Gospel of John: 7:19,23,51; 8:17; 10:34; 15:25.
[3] Instructive examples of Jesus' method will be found in Matthew 5:21-48; 15:1-20; 22:23-33; 22:41-46.
[4] Mark 12:28-34; Matthew 5:17-19. Jesus is addressed as 'Rabbi' chiefly in the Gospel of John (1:38,49; 3:2,26; 6:25) but the title is probably represented by the 'Teacher' and 'Master' of the other Gospels.

depart from the Law was, in Jewish eyes, to depart from the purpose and act of God Himself. So Jesus was bound to reply to the charge, and he did. 'Think not that I came to destroy the Law. I came not to destroy, but to fulfil.'

Nevertheless Christianity eventually broke with Judaism, and with the Law. The Church did retain the books of Moses in its Bible; and Christians are asked to obey such moral precepts as 'Do not steal—do not kill—do not bear false witness.' The ceremonial parts of the Law, however, Christianity does not apply. Now, as we saw, Jesus himself expected a new people to take the place of the old Israel. But did he intend for this new Israel to infringe the laws of Moses—and even discard circumcision, the mark of the covenanted community?

Here is a strange situation. Jesus insisted again and again on the authority of the Law of Moses. Yet both his foes and his followers have seen, in his teaching, bases for setting that Law aside. Certainly, in what it did, the Church has believed that it was following the Master's will. What did Jesus himself do or say, to justify these opinions of him?

First of all, *he made friends of law-violaters.* Few of these were criminals in the modern sense. They were 'publicans and sinners.' A publican was a tax-collector, directly or indirectly in the pay of Rome. Since he got his livelihood by serving the unclean, uncircumcised Gentiles, he was an outcast, excommunicated from synagogue and society. A 'sinner' might sometimes be a felon. More often he was like the donkey driver of Chapter XI: he obeyed parts of the Law but, in the Pharisees' eyes, fell dismally short of his whole duty.

Nothing in the Gospels is more frequently described than Jesus' friendship for the common people, and for the poor, the outcast and the dispossessed. That friendship went back at least to the days of John the Baptist. John, for all the terror of his preaching, had cut through the tangled skein of Pharisaic tradition, pushed aside the mountains of rabbinic interpretation, and struck to the heart of the matter. John's God might not be the loving God of Christianity, but He was a forgiving God. To the man who repented, this God responded directly and immediately. The donkey driver went with his friends to listen to John, and he confessed his sins and got baptized. So when Jesus joined John's movement he thereby aligned himself with the 'am ha-aretz, the people of the land. Always, and in the face of sternest censure, he maintained the alliance.

It is among common people that Christianity was born, and only in this native soil has Christianity ever flourished. When the Church has forgot the rock from whence it was hewn, and has thought first of its own power and prestige, it has grown weak. When the Church has thrown place and perquisites to the winds, and has gone out in compassion to the people of the land, then it has been and always must be strong.

Still, as the Pharisees would no doubt have agreed, a man is known by the company he keeps. Jesus' associates were people who broke the Law. He even sat at table with them. 'He is a glutton and a winebibber,' said the Pharisees. 'He eateth and drinketh with publicans and sinners.' Can we hear the irony in Jesus' reply? 'Those who are well have no need of a physician, but those who are sick.' [5]

Second, while Jesus believed in the Law, obeyed it and cited it constantly, *he introduced a fresh basis for its interpretation.* On the occasion when the disciples got into trouble by plucking grain on the Sabbath, Jesus

[5] Luke 7:34; Mark 2:15-17.

asked their accusers, 'Did ye never read what David did?' Of course they had read it. They and their forebears had wrestled with the story for generations. David was a veritable saint of the Most High, honored by all Israel, and ancestor to the promised Messiah. Yet David had presumed to go into the Temple and eat the shewbread, and serve it to his companions, as though it were a common meal. In any one else the act would have been outrageous sacrilege. Then how could David do it, and remain the great person he so plainly was? Pharisees had discussed it long and furiously, and had erected mountains of explanation that did not explain. Jesus brushed all such questions and answers to one side, and laid bare the heart of the problem. It was the heart, too, of his own concern. David did it *'because he had need.'* It was that simple! Human need is the ground of the Law. It follows that 'the Sabbath was made for man, not man for the Sabbath.' [6]

Human need; then human response to God, not just in outward behavior but in inward attitude: Ye have heard it said, Thou shalt not kill. But *I* say unto you, whosoever hateth is in the same case. Ye have heard it said, Thou shalt not commit adultery. But *I* say unto you, whosoever lusteth is in the same case. Moses because of the hardness of the people's hearts gave them such-and-such a commandment; but from the beginning the demand of the Lord has been for complete purity. Almost we can hear John the Baptist still speaking; for John also had sliced away at the Pharisees' overconfidence, to proclaim a God of justice and forgiveness. But John's God was fearsome; Jesus' God was Father.

The common people heard Jesus gladly. To the Phari-

[6] Matthew 12:1-8; Mark 2:23-28. For David's act, and the law which he transgressed, see I Samuel 21:1-6; Leviticus 24:5-9.

sees, however, he seemed to raise his hand against holy things. Then his treatment of the Law got entangled with their other complaint, that he worked magic. Many of his healings took place on the Sabbath. This was inevitable. To the synagogue came both the strong and the weak, the well and the ill. Those who were ill elicited Jesus' compassionate response. Healing, however, was work, and the Jewish leaders said angrily, 'There are six days in the week for that, but not the seventh!' Jesus answered, 'Would you not on the Sabbath help an ox or an ass that had fallen into a ditch? Is a human being, then, of less worth than an animal?' [7]

So the line was sharply drawn, and there could be no compromise. On one side stood the Pharisees, deeply believing that morality consisted in obeying the letter of the Law, plus the letter of their interpretation; convinced that the written Word defined right and wrong, and that from the definition there was no appeal. On the other side stood Jesus, a loyal Jew, imbued with the Law, but knowing that God's concern is not for the statute but for man himself. Between were the common people to whom, at great cost, Jesus had gone out as to sheep needing a shepherd. These heard him gladly. Yet crowds of that day were not different from crowds of any day, and public faith is seldom constant. The common people themselves were not to be on hand when Jesus needed them most.

> The Law was given through Moses.
> Grace and truth came by Jesus Christ.

So said the author of our Fourth Gospel.[8] One day, seeing the multitudes, Jesus went up a hill and sat down.

[7] See Luke 13:10-17; 14:1-6; Matthew 12:9-14.
[8] John 1:17.

His disciples came to him, and perhaps others came too. He spoke to them; and it was then, Matthew says, that 'he taught them as one having authority, and not as their scribes.' Many of his words on that occasion we have quoted already:

I came not to destroy the Law, but to fulfil it. Ye have heard it said . . . but *I* say. . . . Many will speak to me in that Day, and I will answer. . . . Pray in secret, and your Father, who heareth in secret, will reward you. . . . After this manner pray ye: Our Father. . . . Blessed are the meek, the merciful, the peacemakers, they that hunger and thirst after righteousness.

Here, in the Sermon on the Mount, Jesus promulgated a new Law, from a new mountain.[9] Obedience to it, he said, is of the essence of membership in the Kingdom. The old Law is not destroyed. It is set, rather, into a vast and dizzying understanding of the will of God.

Jesus is Covenant-maker, and he is Law-giver. When he transcended the Law of Moses in the way that he did, it could have just one meaning. A new order was thereby introduced into the world. A new, or at the least, a newly organized people must become the channel of the work of God in history. Law and Covenant both say that.

---

[*] Matthew 5-7. To Jesus' words, as spoken at this time, the author of the First Gospel has evidently added sayings from other occasions. This has not much affected the general outline, however, nor the tenor of Jesus' words. For an earlier stage in the recording of the Sermon, see Parker, *The Gospel Before Mark,* pages 193-195.

CHAPTER XIII

WHAT THE LAW
COULD NOT DO

It will help in the study of this chapter if we first picture a scene. It is of a young man, reading a book, by artificial light.

The light is not like ours today, nor even like those of our great-grandparents. It is more like the lamps in the upper room where Jesus and his companions ate their last supper. It is a shallow pottery dish about as large as the palm of your hand, and it has a beveled edge. On one side a lip or spout has been pinched out, and from this a wick protrudes. The fuel is olive oil. The lamp gives off almost more odor than light. Years hence our reader will have vexing trouble with his eyes. Perhaps his constant reading by lamplight will have contributed to the damage.

His dress, again, differs from ours. He is clothed in the garments of a Pharisee. Though a Pharisee, he is not a typical one. He is better educated, for one thing. He was brought up not here in Palestine, but in a Gentile city. There, besides learning what other Jewish boys learned, he picked up a good deal of information about Greek philosophy and Greek religion. Unlike many Pharisees, he has traveled a good deal. Furthermore, his Pharisaic training itself was under an unusually good teacher.

In still another way, this man stands out from the common run. He is exceedingly intense. He takes life, and himself, very seriously. As a Pharisee, he is certain that man must adhere to the Law of Moses; but he works at it even harder than most. For years, now, he has driven himself without let-up, so as to make sure that God will accept him. If God has accepted a man, the man's mind ought to be at peace. To this man, however, peace of mind has not come. He does not know why. His only remedy is to push all the harder. Day after day he strains to follow every tiny injunction in the Law and in Pharisaic tradition. He *must* know the will of God, and do it. Sometimes he is almost frantic about it.

The book he is reading does not look like a modern book. Instead of pages hinged at the back, there are columns inscribed on a continuous roll. The book is in Hebrew, a language written from right to left. As he reads, he unwinds with his left and winds with his right. But while the book is unlike ours in language and shape, the difference ends there. The words that he is reading most of us have read too. He has read them before, so often that he knows them by heart.

'Thou shalt have no other gods before me.' No! No more than any other Jew, would he dream of acknowledging any god but the God of Israel.

'Thou shalt not make unto thee any graven image.' He has obeyed that also. Not many years ago there had been a bloody riot when Pilate tried to bring the Roman national standard into Jerusalem. It was an 'image,' and the Jews would not have it in the Holy City. Our young reader had, of course, approved his fellow-Jews' stand.

'Thou shalt not take the Name of the Lord thy God in

vain.' 'Remember that thou keep holy the Sabbath day.' He had obeyed these to the letter, and he was steeped in the Pharisees' interpretations of them.

'Thou shalt not kill, nor commit adultery, nor steal, nor bear false witness.' He had refrained from all these evil acts. He could have said with the rich young ruler, 'All these commandments have I kept from my youth up.' [1] Then how could peace elude him so long? Must there be no end to this driving, burning, fruitless effort? No assurance of the favor of God? 'What lack I yet?'

Suddenly a sentence leaped from the column. He had read it a thousand times, yet it flashed as though he had never seen it before, and it seared into his mind. THOU SHALT NOT COVET.

For the first time, Saul of Tarsus understood, and it was the bitterest defeat he would ever know. This Law, this holy Word of very God, required of him what he could never do. Not only must he refrain from evil behavior. He must have no evil desires—never for an instant wish for a thing or a place that was not rightfully his. His long and frenzied search had been in vain. You must—you can't—you can't—you must! He could never obey. He would never know peace in his soul. He was caught. Years afterward he wrote of this moment: 'Then sin revived, and I died.—Oh wretched man that I am, who shall deliver me from this body of death?' [2]

There was an answer, but in finding it Saul, whom we know better as Paul, became a Christian. [3] Before study-

---

[1] The story of the rich young ruler is told in Matthew 19:16-22; Mark 10:17-22; Luke 18:18-23. Some people have surmised that he and the hero of this chapter were the same person—but that is sheer guesswork.
[2] Romans 7:9,24.
[3] It is sometimes said that Saul the Jew became Paul the Christian. Actually, however, we do not know when he took the name 'Paul.' The word means 'little,' and may have been his nickname years before his conversion.

ing the answer, we must see clearly just what the problem of the Law was, as Saul/Paul faced it.

His difficulty stemmed initially from his love for the Law. Had he not revered it so much, he might simply have slighted it—as, under the pressures of Gentile civilization, some Jews did. Saul of Tarsus could not. 'The Law,' he said, 'is true and righteous and good,' and he insisted on that to the end of his life. When some opponents charged that he set the Law aside, he denied it hotly. 'Do we make the Law of none effect? No! We establish the Law.' 'Or are ye ignorant, brethren (for I speak to men who know the Law), that the Law hath dominion over a man for so long a time as he liveth?' [4] The Law is the utterance, the actual syllables, of God Himself, and is the measure by which man's moral deeds are to be measured.

As Paul's high regard for the Law never waned, neither did his Jewishness. He did welcome Gentile converts into the Church, and evidently he loved them deeply. Still, he nearly always addressed them with a certain condescension, as though he had a more fortunate origin. While they shared without stint in the tree of life, they were an 'engrafted branch.' 'What advantage hath the Jew? Much in every way.' He spoke of 'Israelites, whose is the glory, and the covenants, and the Law, and the promises . . . and of whom is Christ.' Proudly he asserted that he himself was 'a Hebrew of the Hebrews; as touching the Law, a Pharisee.' [5]

Yet it was the very goodness of the Law that was man's undoing. This came about in two ways. First and most

[4] Romans 3:31; 7:1. The expression here rendered 'No!' is Greek *mē genoito* ('may it not be') which has the force of 'not at all,' 'by no means.' In some Bibles it is represented by the sixteenth-century English idiom 'God forbid,' though neither 'God' nor 'forbid' is in the original.
[5] Romans 11:13-24; 3:1-2; 9:4-5; Philippians 3:4-6.

important, the Law defines sin in the way that God defines it. Thus it makes sinfulness stark and horrible. Without this measuring rod, man would not have known how far short he fell. Now he knows.

Second, the Law arouses a devilish perversity in human nature. Just because there is a commandment, I feel a desire to assert myself and disobey. 'I perceive,' said Paul, 'a "law" in my members, at war with the Law of my mind. For the evil that I know to be evil, that I do. And the good that I know to be good, that I do not.' [6]

The Law itself is powerless to overcome these evil effects. It can say what good is—but it cannot make us good. It tells us where we have done wrong against the infinite God—but it leaves us without means to expiate that wrong or to counterbalance it. It shows us how sorely we need the forgiveness of God—but it does not provide forgiveness, nor can it guarantee it. Good, holy and just, it proves to me that I can never be good or holy or just ('Thou shalt not covet!') and so it leaves me in despair.

It might seem that the Gentile, who does not know the Law of Moses, would not face this appalling dilemma. However, the Gentile does know some law. He can deduce it from the world about him, for God has not left Himself without a witness, of some sort, anywhere in the world. The Gentile too has learned that truth is better than falsehood, kindness better than cruelty, wisdom better than stupidity, faithfulness better than treachery. Yet the Gentile has disobeyed the law he does know.

It is the Jew, however, who with all his advantages is in the worst case of all. He knows the whole Law and cannot plead ignorance. Therefore he has amongst all people the heaviest responsibility, and faces the greatest

[6] See Romans 7:19-23.

condemnation for lawbreaking. This was St. Paul's devastating answer to those Jews who, because of their Covenant and their custodianship of the Law, thought they would get more divine favor than the Gentiles.

Every person in the world is in the same case. Every person knows, partly anyhow, what is good. Every one does (and likes!) what he knows to be evil. An offender, he can never offer redress unless Some One, not himself, provides it. A slave to evil, he will never be free unless Some One, not himself, frees him. The matter, as Paul saw it, is very much as Jesus put it in the Sermon on the Mount. There, too, a moral scale is set up in which, when man is weighed, he is always found wanting. I am never so kind, or selfless, or loving, or sincere, or truthful, or peaceable, as I know I ought to be. I need the Father's forgiveness. Only the Father can provide that.

Here another question interposed itself. Is not God unfair, to place upon man demands which He knows man cannot fulfil? To Paul the question was an impertinence, and he answered with a sharp 'No!' God is absolute Sovereign and we, finite creatures, may not question His way of governing His world. Yet, it is clear, the hard commandments of the Law do serve a divine purpose. By their means God demonstrates how incomplete man is, how man needs help, and how that help *must* come from divine love since man has no way to purchase it.

The initiative lies with the Most High. And precisely here is where Christianity comes in. *God has taken the initiative*. The way out of man's predicament, which man himself could never have provided, God has supplied. Paul says this so often and in so many ways that it is like a refrain in his writings:[7]

[7] The following quotations are again abridged, and it would be worth while to look up their contexts in the New Testament. See Galatians 3:15-4:31; II Corinthians 5:17-19; Philippians 3:3-14.

Before faith came, we were kept in ward under the Law, so that the Law was our tutor to bring us unto Christ. But now that faith has come, we are no longer under a tutor. For ye are all children of God through faith in Christ Jesus.

If any man is in Christ, he is a new creature. The old things are passed away; behold, they are become new. All things are of God, who reconciled us to himself through Christ. God was in Christ, reconciling the world unto himself.

I count all things to be loss for the excellency of the knowledge of Christ Jesus my Lord: that I may be found in him, not having a righteousness of mine own which is of the Law, but that which is through faith in Christ, the righteousness which is from God by faith.

One is reminded of the passages, quoted in Chapter IX, where New Testament writers declared that the New Age had already begun.[8] Here, however, Paul's emphasis is different and more specific: *God has acted to free us from our dilemma.* To this divine act Paul applies various names. For his most important term there is a very fortunate English equivalent: *atonement,* i.e., *at-one-ment* with God. By His act, God enables man to be *at one* with Him.

Now it is one thing (a) to recognize the fact, that through Jesus' death and resurrection people have been reunited to God. It is quite another thing (b) to explain how this reunion comes about.

(a) The facts, the data with which St. Paul dealt, were that the Son of God had lived, died, and risen again; and that in those events Paul found a release for his spirit, an assurance of God's favor, and a conscious union with his fellowmen, that he had previously sought in vain. His converts found the same thing, and so have Christians ever since. The transformation that comes from Jesus'

[8] Above, pages 82ff.

death and resurrection is no mere private religiosity or 'funny internal feeling.' In a most important sense, Christianity would be true whether anybody believed it or not. It is *God's act*, objective, external, *there*. It means that something new has been added to the world, a new Covenant, new Law, new reality. To be Christian is to perceive, to recognize that new thing.

(b) Yet *how* did Jesus bring this atonement about? Was man's life 'forfeit' (to God? to the Devil?) and did Jesus give his life to 'redeem the forfeit?' Did Jesus become a substitute for us, taking the punishment which we otherwise should have got? Did mankind so offend God that God could be propitiated only by the sacrifice of this holy victim? Did man's sin against the Infinite One throw the universe so out of kilter that God Himself must die to redress the balance? Did Christ tender a ransom to the Devil and then, by his resurrection, cheat the Devil out of it? Or is it just that when we think about Jesus we are deeply stirred, and moved to mend our ways and turn to God?

Every one of these suggestions has been urged, and stoutly defended, during the past nineteen centuries. Each of them may contain elements of truth. Nearly all of them, however, require us to speculate about matters on which we cannot possibly have enough knowledge. St. Paul's own explanation was of a different sort. For it he drew on some familiar religious symbols of his day. To grasp what he said, therefore, we must first glance at some features of Greek religion in the ancient world.

If the Jew's greatest question was, 'When will Messiah come?', the Greek had a more difficult and paralyzing problem. It was the problem of death. He looked for an eternal soul within man; but either he found none, or at best he could not be sure. Does life have permanent significance? Is death the defeat of all that we have done, the final frustration whose sardonic humor the universe itself is too dead to laugh at? All of us have asked such questions. Perhaps, at times, we have been tempted to agree with the English chappie who sang,

> Now there's really nothing in it, don't you know?
> We are living for the minute, don't you know?
> You are born, and then you cry.
> You grow older, and you sigh—
> Older still, and then you die, don't you know?

The young, intelligent Greek had searched in many quarters for an answer. He had tried Homeric religion, the ancient myths of the gods on Mt. Olympus. By this time, of course, educated people no longer believed in the literal truth of that religion. One might try, however, to reinterpret it, using the old tales to teach new ideas. Yet a religion is deathly ill when people have stopped believing its content, and revere only its formulas; or when people try to load the mere words with meanings they were never intended to bear. Let the best intellects construe it as they might, Homeric religion could not long satisfy the alert and searching first century mind.

Then there was philosophy. Plato, for example, had argued that man is immortal, and to many his reasoning seemed conclusive. At best, however, intellectual conviction is not enough, for life is not transformed by a mere Q. E. D. Drive a man into a corner where he can think of no reply, and you do not thereby give him a faith to live by. Religious argument has its place, certainly. It can show that faith is not unreasonable, and thus, as it were, 'lead the horse to the trough.' It cannot make him drink.

So the Greek had tried what are known as mystery religions. These were secret cults and we do not know all their details, though their general nature is clear enough.

A mystery cult was devoted to one of the lesser deities, like Osiris or Mithra. There were initiation ceremonies, such as getting baptized in the blood of a bull. Then there might be a sacred meal, shared by all the adherents and, supposedly, by the god himself. In these and other esoteric ways, the devotee tried to *merge his life with the life of the immortal god*. Then the worshipper, who could not guarantee his own life after death, would be carried forward into immortality by the god to whom he was joined.

Now Greek culture had spread all over the Mediterranean area, and far to the eastward, and the Greek language was spoken everywhere. (That is, of course, why the New Testament was written in Greek rather than in Jesus' mother tongue.) Mystery cults too had spread far and wide, and they influenced the thought and the language of the whole first century world. In explaining Christianity to the minds of Africa, Asia Minor, Greece or Italy, early Christians were bound to use this Greek religious vocabulary.

St. Paul saw, however, that more than words were involved here. The idea of a divine figure, doing for us what we cannot do for ourselves, has a universal appeal. Even Buddhism has tales of a man who accumulated so much merit that others, less worthy, could draw on his store. Closer home, the unknown prophet of the Exile had told of the Servant on whom the iniquities of mankind were laid, and who suffered vicariously for 'us all.' [9] The mystery cults were groping after a real truth. There is One with whom we may unite ourselves firmly. Such union will bring eternal life, and establish us for ever in complete assurance.

Sometimes this aspiration had been expressed in noble

[9] See above, pages 39-41.

ways. At other times, on the contrary, mystery cult practices were grossly revolting. Whether noble or debased,
however, they expressed merely an idea in people's minds
or a longing of their hearts. But now, said St. Paul, what
was once a concept has become a fact, an objective, living reality. Within his own lifetime there lived one with
whom men really can unite their lives, and who really
does 'bring life and immortality to light.' Here was indeed
a solution to the Greek's problem of death!—no myth or
syllogism or mystification, but a concrete event. This
Christ lived, and died, and rose from death.

In the atonement we merge our lives with Christ's, so
that we too, as it were, die and rise again. For Paul this
was not a theory, or a poetic image, but the most intensely real experience. 'It is no longer I that live, but
Christ liveth in me.' 'The life that I now live, I live by
faith in the Son of God, who loved me and gave himself
up for me.' 'For me, to live is Christ.'[10]

The dying-and-rising process Paul illustrated in many
ways. One very important figure was baptism. In those
days Christian baptism was by immersion—dipping the
entire body into the water—as is the case in some de-
nominations today. In thus going down and coming up
again, said Paul, the convert reënacts the burial and rising
of Christ. He does more. He makes Christ's death and
resurrection his own, for he himself dies to sin and rises
to newness of life.[11] Another illustration Paul used was
that of the widow. So long as her husband lives she is
bound to him, but his death breaks the tie. St. Paul was
less skillful in story-telling than the Master, and here he

---

[10] See Galatians 2:20; Philippians 1:21.
[11] Some people have misunderstood Paul's discussion (Romans 6:3-11)
to be a teaching about baptism. It is not. It is a teaching about the
atonement, for which baptism is a figure.

leaves some doubt as to which figure is which.[12] If the widow represents the Christian, then the former way of life is dead and the Christian is free to 'marry' Christ. If the husband represents the Christian, then the latter has himself died to the old life and risen to the new. Despite the confusion, the basic lessons are plain: (1) Christianity means union with Christ himself. (2) Christianity differs from non-Christianity as life differs from death.

In all this, said St. Paul, the Christian is 'made righteous' or 'justified.' Does Paul mean by this that the Christian has goodness 'infused' into him so that he loses his freedom, and has to be good willy-nilly? Put that way the statement is, of course, absurd, and St. Paul would not have held with it. Yet just as a planet shines not by its own light but by the light of the sun, so the Christian 'shines' not by his own goodness, but by reflecting the goodness of God—'not having mine own righteousness, which is of the Law, but that which is through faith in Christ, the righteousness which is from God by faith' (*Philippians* 3:9). *Freedom of choice, however, and full responsibility for our own acts, are as real as ever.* St. Paul brings this out in countless injunctions:[13]

I beseech you, brethren, to present your bodies a living sacrifice, holy, acceptable unto God. And be not fashioned according to this world: but be transformed by the renewing of your mind, that ye may prove what is the will of God.

Let us not judge one another any more: but judge ye this rather, that no man put a stumblingblock in his brother's way.

Now I beseech you [Church members at Corinth] that ye all speak the same thing, and that there be no divisions among you.

[12] Romans 7:2-4.
[13] Romans 12:1-2; 14:13; I Corinthians 1:10; Galatians 5:25-6:10; Colossians 3:5-17.

If we live by the Spirit, by the Spirit let us also walk. Let us not become vainglorious, provoking one another, envying one another. Brethren, even if a man be overtaken in a fault, ye who are spiritual restore such a one in a spirit of gentleness; looking to thyself, lest thou also be tempted.

Uncleanness, evil desire, covetousness, wherein ye also once walked, when ye lived in these things; but now, put them all aside. Lie not one to another; seeing ye have put off the old man with his doings, and have put on the new man that is being renewed unto knowledge after the image of him that created him.

St. Paul does not say, 'You have died to sin; so you cannot sin.' He says, 'You have died to sin; so *do not* sin.'

Then does 'justification' mean that goodness is 'imputed' to us? Are we acquitted before the bar of divine justice, and thereafter treated as though we had not done what, in fact, we did do? To many, that sounds like a legal fiction to which the God of Truth could not be a party. On a higher level, however, it is not a fiction. It is forgiveness. When you have forgiven some one, you do not have to pretend, nor do you lose your memory. You restore the offender to full relationship with yourself. If you have really forgiven him, his offense can never again rise between you, and your friendship is as free and warm as it had ever been. (So if some one says, 'Oh yes, I forgive him, but . . .' he has not forgiven at all.) Only the person who has never forgiven, nor been forgiven, can suppose that forgiveness is a pretense or a fiction. It costs. This is what St. Paul meant by justification. It is what Jesus meant when he told of a prodigal son, and of the father who ran to meet him.[14]

St. Paul uses other words to describe this act of God and our response to it. Only two of them need detain us here. One is *grace*. This means the love and favor of God

[14] Luke 15:11-32.

whereby He, the Almighty and Infinite, has condescended to meet man's need. Some one has said that in its combination of lilting sound and thrilling meaning, 'grace' is the most beautiful word in English. Yet that God, *the* God, should thus stoop to us is a thought so awe-inspiring, so rousing, that 'beautiful' is not enough.

> Love so amazing, so divine,
> Demands my soul, my life, my all.

The other word is *faith*. Nowadays this term is used in many ways. When one says, 'I have faith in him,' 'faith' means 'confidence.' On the other hand, when one says, 'I kept faith with him,' one means, 'I was loyal' or 'trustworthy.' Sometimes, again, 'faith' is applied to a set of beliefs, such as are stated in a creed. Or it may mean a whole religion, as when we speak loosely of 'the Mohammedan faith' or 'the Mormon faith.'

For St. Paul, 'faith' had still another, much richer meaning. It stood for the Christian life itself, a whole-souled acceptance of what God has done, 'a divinely-wrought, loving, and hearty reliance upon God,' as one dictionary puts it. Here once more, Paul comes close to Jesus' own interpretation. For Jesus, 'to have faith' meant to appropriate the gift of God actively and confidently, and to apply it to the enrichment of daily life.

By this faith, then, man takes God's gracious act of atonement and makes it his own; and he is assured that God forgives him. *That* is what, for so many years under the Law, Saul of Tarsus had looked for and had not found. When he found it in Christianity, the Law was not thereby deposed; but it was seen to be only a part of the whole truth. This whole truth, St. Paul now saw, was broader and more enthralling than he had ever dreamed. So, said he, the 'works of the Law' do not avail. God has cut across them, and His act *does* avail.

Not every one, not even every Christian, grasped Paul's meaning right away. The *Epistle of James* seems deliberately to argue against Paul when it says, 'Faith without works is dead. Show me thy faith apart from thy works, and I will show thee my faith by my works. Thou believest that God is one? Thou doest well. But the demons also believe, and shudder!' (*James 2:14,17-20*) If these words were directed against Paul, as many scholars think, then their author knew only a caricature of Paul's own teachings. (Perhaps he learned about Paul's ideas at second- or third-hand.) With Paul himself, as we saw, faith meant the full Christian life, and works meant legalistic, ceremonial efforts to appease God. In James, faith means assent to a creed, and works means kindliness, love, unselfishness, and obeying all the other commands of Christ. Now ceremony and creed are important to Christianity, as two thousand years of history plainly show. Nevertheless, Paul's conception of faith is richer than James', while James' conception of works is richer than Paul's.

The long search was over. The defeat of that bitter night, when Saul first realized he could never obey, was turned into such a victory as the non-Christian, whether Jew or pagan, could never know. The Law, that wonderful and holy thing, had brought chagrin and despair, but

There is now no condemnation to them that are in Christ Jesus. For the Law of the Spirit of life in Christ Jesus made me free from the Law of sin and death. For what the Law [of Moses] could not do, in that it was weak through the flesh, God sending his own Son in the likeness of sinful flesh, and for sin, condemned sin in the flesh.

What then shall we say to these things? If God be for us, who can be against us? He that spared not his own Son, but delivered him up for us all, how shall he not also with him freely give us all things? Who shall lay anything to the charge of God's chosen ones? It is God that justifieth: who is he that condemneth? It is Christ Jesus that died, yea rather that is risen from the dead.

Nay, in all these things we are more than conquerors through him that loved us. For I am persuaded that neither death, nor life, nor angels, nor principalities, nor things present, nor things to come, nor powers, nor height, nor depth, nor any other creature, shall be able to separate us from the love of God, which is in Christ Jesus our Lord.[15]

[15] Romans 8. Again, read the whole chapter!

CHAPTER XIV

THE FIRST CHRISTIAN SCHISM

This chapter is about an argument that split the Church in two, nearly two thousand years ago. The question was, What is the right relation of Christianity to Judaism? In order to be a Christian,[1] must one first become a Jew, that is, be circumcised and obey all the Law of Moses? Today we readily answer No, astonished perhaps that the question is even asked. Yet at one time 'No' was an exceedingly difficult answer to give. Some of the most sincere and devoted Christians were sure that, to accept Messiah, one must accept the Israel for whom Messiah came. Indeed this was so obvious that it did not occur to them to discuss it, until the issue was forced upon them.

Those who demanded that Gentile converts first become Jews are called *Judaizers*. To a modern mind the Judaizers' point of view is novel, and we had best see what a strong case they really had. Jesus himself had been a Jew, 'circumcised the eighth day' and reared in strict conformity with the Law of Moses. While he offered new understandings of the Law, he never once stepped outside the Jewish faith. He appealed constantly to the Torah. He accepted the title of Rabbi. He said, 'Not a

[1] The word 'Christian' did not come into use right away (see Acts 11:26). The movement was at first known as 'the Way' or 'the Nazorean sect.' In the present discussion, however, it is simpler to use 'Christian' all the way through.

jot or tittle shall pass from the Law. He who keeps its commandments shall be called great in the Kingdom of Heaven. He who breaks its slightest injunction shall be called least in the Kingdom.' He had aided one or two Gentile parents, to be sure, yet he had expressly declared that he 'was sent only to the lost sheep of the house of Israel.' He enjoined his disciples similarly, 'Go not into any way of the Gentiles, but go only to the lost sheep of the house of Israel.'

Furthermore the Christian claim was, precisely, that Jesus fulfilled the Jewish Scriptures. The very word 'Christ' or 'Messiah' came from those Scriptures. Indeed Judaism gave the New Testament writers every phrase they ever used about Jesus: second Adam, Lamb of God, Priest for ever after the order of Melchizedek, Servant of the Lord, Son of man. Jesus' own teaching was rooted, as we ourselves have seen, in the Covenant thinking of the Old Testament. For a long time, the Old Testament would be the only Bible Christianity had.

Then most of the Judaizers came from Palestine. Some had been Jesus' own disciples or, like James 'the brother of the Lord,' members of his family.[2] They could claim with much justice that they knew more about their Master's intentions than any late-comer to Christianity was likely to know.

The earliest Christians, who were closest to Jesus in time and place, certainly acted as though the Judaizers'

[2] Jesus' 'brothers and sisters' may have been children of Joseph by a previous marriage. Jesus was Mary's firstborn, yet in the Gospels his 'brothers' treat him disrespectfully, as though he were younger than themselves. At the Crucifixion, the Fourth Gospel says that Jesus gave Mary to the care of one of his disciples, which would be strange if she had other children on whom to lean. Also, Joseph never appears with Mary after Jesus is grown. This fits the surmise that Joseph, being older than Mary, had died; and this in turn would make it likely that Joseph was married before.

The foregoing is of course no proof, but at best a reasonable supposition.

point of view were the right one. The history of this primitive Church is told in the *Book of Acts*. St. Luke, who wrote *Acts*, did not agree with the Judaizers, and he would not have emphasized their attitude more than was merited. Yet he says that these early Christians worshipped faithfully in the Temple, kept the Jewish feasts, and appealed to the Law of Moses. Their leaders preached that persons 'outside the Law' (that is, Gentiles) had killed Jesus. The new movement made multitudes of converts in Palestine, including not a few Pharisees, and Luke describes them as 'all zealous for the Law.' [3]

In this wall of Jewishness, which surrounded the early Church, some cracks appeared. At first they did not amount to much. St. Stephen was arrested on a charge of violating the Law. Luke says, however, that Stephen was not guilty; and he got stoned only after he charged the Jewish leaders themselves with breaking the Law (*Acts 6:8-7:60*). Peter was told, in a vision, to eat food that the Law forbade. But up to that time, at least, he had not done such a thing nor had he understood Jesus to recommend it. Because of his vision, Peter visited a Gentile home and baptized some uncircumcised Romans. That got him into serious trouble with the rest of the Jerusalem Church, and there is no record in Acts of his repeating the 'offense.' [4] At *Acts 11:20* some editions of the Bible say that Jewish Christian leaders preached to Greeks. The better New Testament manuscripts read not 'Greeks' however, but 'Greek-speaking Jews.' [5]

[3] The story of the Jewish Christian Church occupies most of Acts 1:1 to 13:46. Striking instances of the Judaizing viewpoint are to be found at 2:1,46; 3:1ff.,22-23; 5:12,21,42; 6:7; also 15:5 and 21:20.
[4] However, Peter's explanation of his act did satisfy at least some of the Jerusalem Church leaders. The whole incident is recounted in Acts 10:9-11:18.
[5] Before printing was invented in the 15th century, all New Testament books were copied toilsomely by hand. Thousands of variations in read-

The situation among these earliest Jewish Christians is plain. They thought of themselves as good Jews. They were in fact better Jews than their fellow-countrymen because they knew who Messiah was, and followed him; and because they were blessed with the Spirit of the Lord. In their preaching they pointed to Jesus himself, his words and the events of his life; and to the Hebrew Scriptures which he so patently fulfilled.

Into this situation entered Saul of Tarsus. First he came as a persecutor. There was in Jerusalem a Jewish council known as the *Sanhedrin*. It had legal authority only in and near Jerusalem, but its prestige extended much farther than that and its decisions were heeded by devout Jews everywhere. The Sanhedrin appointed Saul to harry the Christian movement and to try to stamp it out. They commissioned him to go to Damascus. On the way there, in the heat of the noon-day sun Saul had an overwhelming experience. The Lord Jesus appeared to him and talked with him. He was converted. The religion he had hated was now his own.[6]

Paul brought many gifts to Christianity. Perhaps the most valuable, at just that time, was his intellect. He was not the first educated man to be converted: other Pharisees had preceded him. Church leadership, however, had been in the hands of a few men whom Acts calls 'unlearned and ignorant.' They were full of zeal and devotion, but they could not give to their new-found faith the cogent reasoning and careful formulation that it needed. Paul was equipped to do so, even more than

ing crept in. Most of them were trivial—changes in spelling, replacing the original word with a synonym, etc. A few, like the present one, involve real difference of meaning. Not one affects the content of the Christian faith.
[6] The story of Paul's conversion is told three times in Acts, with slight variations: 9:1-18; 22:1-16; 26:9-20.

most Pharisees. Part of his contribution we examined in the last chapter.

Consider now the logical outcome of Paul's reasoning. The Law, righteous and good and holy, still is unable either to stop wrongdoing or to bring divine forgiveness. Christ by his atonement has done both; and this new life and this forgiveness are made available through our faith. Christ has, in effect, short-circuited the Law, both the Mosaic Law of the Jews and the natural law of the Gentiles. In other words, Christ's atonement accomplishes the whole purpose of the Law. Every one, who has faith in Christ, achieves everything the Law offered, and in a better way than the Law could possibly do. Therefore Gentiles, by believing in Christ, accomplish everything the Law provides. Therefore *Gentiles may come directly into Messiah's Kingdom, and need not go through Jewish ceremonial.*

Paul knew the Scriptures. He knew how to use them in ways that were effective with his contemporaries. For example, he quoted the saying, 'There is none righteous, no, not one.' [7] This, he said, means that no one is guiltless before the Law; hence no one can expect salvation through the Law. Again he recalled the early covenant that was made with Abraham. This took place, Paul reminded his readers, before Abraham was circumcised, and solely on the ground of Abraham's faith. Therefore the true sons of Abraham are not necessarily those with a particular physical characteristic, but are those who share Abraham's faith.[8] In Hebrew lore, after Moses talked with God his face shone so brightly that people could not look at him, and Moses had to wear a veil. Israel, said Paul, has kept a veil between itself and the right understanding

[7] Psalm 14:3; Romans 3:10.
[8] Romans 3:21-4:25; Galatians 3:6-18; 4:21-5:6.

of Moses' Law. 'But we [followers of Christ] all, with unveiled face, beholding as in a mirror the glory of the Lord, are transformed into the same image, from glory to glory.' (*II Corinthians 3*) Paul's letters contain scores of discussions like these.

Both logic and his own experience had persuaded Paul that Christianity was too vast a thing for the narrow limits of Jewish national religion. Uncircumcised Gentiles must be admitted into the Church on equal footing with circumcised Jews. There was, no doubt, a less illustrious reason for his conviction. In preaching to Jews, Paul was not a success. Perhaps he was too intense to suit the ordinary people of Palestine. Perhaps his ideas were too abstruse, or his words and illustrations, drawn from experience in other lands, too unfamiliar. Perhaps his hearers distrusted and resented his sudden conversion to Christianity. Whatever it was, his results in Palestine were meagre. In contrast, the other apostles, though harassed by the Sanhedrin, were a huge success with the common people. They made converts by three thousand at a stroke, or five thousand, or myriads.[9] When Paul tried the same kind of preaching, either the Jews would not listen or, sometimes, they drove him out of town. In exasperation he finally said to a group of them, 'It was necessary that the word of God should first be spoken to you. Seeing ye thrust it from you, and judge yourselves unworthy of eternal life, lo, we turn to the Gentiles!' (*Acts 13:46*) These words are at the exact mid-point of *Acts*, and they are the turning point of the whole book.

What would have been the story of Christianity, had Paul been more popular with his own people! Does it not seem that God used the weakness of this man to change the history of the world?

[9] Acts 2:41,47; 4:4; 21:20.

Yet Paul may have seemed less prominent in the first century than he does to us. We know him through his letters and the *Book of Acts*, but these were published only after his death. Superbly as he argued the case for the Gentile converts, he was not the only advocate they had. His view was shared in varying degrees by Barnabas, Silas, the author of our Second Gospel, and others. Peter vacillated at first, but eventually came round to Paul's position. While Peter cannot have got to Rome as early as some people think,[10] he certainly went there eventually, and probably died under the Emperor Nero. The pro-Gentile conviction was not easy for any of these leaders. It seems to have followed their astonished discovery that Gentiles, like Jews, could show signs of the presence of the Spirit of God. Perhaps, also, it was fostered by a large number of Greek-speaking Jews who early joined the Christian movement. These were loyal Jews, but they had a broader outlook than their Aramaic-speaking brethren; and it is evident from *Acts* that the two groups did not work well together.

So the issue was joined. On one side were the leaders of the Jerusalem Church, many of whom had spent years with Jesus himself. When they first heard that unclean, uncircumcised Gentiles were infesting the Messiah's Kingdom, it filled them with horror. Some felt that such a catastrophe must mean that the end of the world was coming! On the other side stood St. Paul, with a handful of supporters most of whom had, like himself, come late into Christianity. Paul saw how big Christianity was, and that it must burst the shell of the parent faith. The en-

[10] Some traditions put him in Rome in A.D. 42. But according to Galatians 2, he was still in Jerusalem for some years after that. When Paul wrote the epistle to the Romans in A.D. 57, he gave no sign that Peter had yet gone to that city.

suing struggle first rocked and then split the Church. No schism since then, not even the Protestant Reformation, was more fateful.

When the Jerusalem leaders first heard of the Gentile newcomers, it is to their credit that they tried a compromise. An analogy lay ready to hand. In Chapter XIII we saw how Greeks were looking for a satisfying religion. Many of them thought they found it in Judaism. They did not like the Jewish initiatory rite, and the translation of the Hebrew Bible made absurd Greek. Still, the religion offered a God Who cared about man's moral nature; and it provided religious activities that extended from the synagogue into the home, and from the cradle to the grave. Therefore many Gentiles took to attending synagogue services and to obeying so much of the Law as they could without becoming Jews. (They even kept the Passover.) They were given the name of 'God-fearers.' When in *Acts* St. Paul begins a speech, 'Ye men of Israel and *ye that fear God*,' he is using this technical term.[11] The Christian leaders held a council in Jerusalem. During the meeting, James 'the brother of the Lord' suggested that the Church welcome Gentiles on the same basis that the synagogues did, asking them only to give alms and to abstain from forbidden food. James' proposal carried the day.[12]

The compromise could not last, for it did not touch the deep convictions which separated the two sides. A group of Judaizers once trailed Paul through the towns of Asia Minor. They told his converts that he was not a true Apostle, that he had no right to speak for Christ or the

[11] Acts 13:16. See also the description of Cornelius, Acts 10:2ff.
[12] See Acts 15:6-29. It may be this same Council that is discussed by Paul in Galatians 2, though the descriptions differ somewhat.

Church; that, contrary to what Paul had told them, they *must* become Jews and obey the Law of Moses. Some of them were won over. When the news reached Paul he dictated an epistle to the Galatians, which is one of the sharpest letters of Christian history. The opening follows the conventional pattern for letters of the time except that, in his agitation, Paul fails to say that he prays for his readers. Such a declaration would have been normal, and it appears in all of Paul's letters except this one.

Paul, an apostle not from men, neither through man, but through Jesus Christ, and God the Father who raised him from the dead. . . .

Unto the churches of Galatia: Grace to you and peace from God. . . .

I marvel that ye are so quickly removing from him that called you in the grace of Christ unto a different gospel. . . . But though we, or an angel from heaven, should preach unto you any gospel other than that which we preached unto you, let him be anathema. . . .

O foolish Galatians, who hath bewitched you?

He went on to tell how he was converted to Christianity, and of his early experiences in the new faith. He reviewed the reaction of the Jerusalem Church to his work, and how its leaders had not forbidden him to go to the Gentiles. He described Simon Peter's changeableness. It is the most autobiographical of St. Paul's letters. It is also, next to *Romans,* the strongest statement of his whole religious position.

The Jewish Christians who challenged Paul's authority sincerely felt that he was an upstart and a perverter of the Way. True, the Jerusalem leaders early gave him the right hand of fellowship, and Paul took this as an endorsement of his task. Then in Antioch he and Barnabas were commissioned, by the laying on of hands, to their missionary work.[13] Still the Jerusalem leaders did not win other Jewish Christians to Paul's view, and probably they did not try. All through his ministry Paul had to defend his right to speak. That is why he so often began a letter insistently, 'Paul, an *apostle* of Jesus Christ.' He appealed chiefly not to his commission from the other Church leaders, but to that from Jesus himself: 'Am I not an apostle? Have not I seen the Lord?' 'Christ appeared to all the apostles, and last of all to me also.' 'I was not disobedient unto the heavenly vision.' [14] In the heat of the controversy he played down his debt to the other apostles, and spoke of them harshly. This was especially true in Galatians, but it appears elsewhere, notably in *II Corinthians 11:4-6*:

For if he that cometh preacheth another Jesus whom we did not preach, or a different gospel, which ye did not accept, ye do well to bear with him. For I reckon that I am not a whit behind those preëminent apostles. But though I be rude in speech, yet am I not in knowledge.

On returning to Jerusalem for the last time, Paul was warned by the Jerusalem leaders of the Church. Although they trusted him, they said, he was under suspicion among the mass of Jewish Christians. They advised him to prove his Jewishness by offering a sacrifice in the Temple. Paul consented. When he went to the Temple, however, rumor got out that he had taken an uncircumcised Gentile into the area reserved for Jews. A riot started and the Roman captain, not knowing what the disturbance was about, arrested Paul. Jewish opponents preferred all sorts of charges against him, most of which meant little to a Roman officer. So, partly for Paul's own

[13] Acts 13:2-3. This is the one point where, it might be argued, other Christian leaders *ordained* Paul. But Paul said that he, like the other apostles, had been ordained directly by Jesus himself. See Galatians 1:1, and quotations given below.
[14] I Corinthians 9:1; 15:7-8; Acts 26:19.

protection, he was imprisoned in Caesarea on the coast.[15] There he languished for two years, with one hearing after another, but getting nowhere.

Finally he fell back on his right as a Roman citizen. Roman citizenship was a legal status, which Paul had inherited. It offered prerogatives and dignities not otherwise available. Even if condemned to death, a Roman citizen faced beheading and not crucifixion. Jesus, of course, had had no such status. Paul did have, and with his citizenship he had a right. He appealed to Caesar. Then came the ultimate irony. Had he not appealed to Caesar, he was told, he would have been released. Now, however, he must go to Rome.[16] So in fetters Paul finally reached the city he had longed to see. There he was under a kind of house arrest, chained to a guard but permitted to occupy his own quarters, receive guests, and employ note-takers to write letters for him. In Rome he again preached to Jews, but again he failed. Again, therefore, he said to them,

Well spake the Holy Spirit through Isaiah unto your fathers, saying, This people's heart is waxed gross, and their ears are dull of hearing, and their eyes have they closed . . . Be it known therefore unto you, that this salvation of God is sent unto the Gentiles. They will hear. (*Acts 28:17-29*)

The *Book of Acts* stops there. It may indeed have been written as a kind of brief for Paul's defense before the Emperor. We do not know how his case turned out. Ancient literature contains some hints—they are no more than hints—that he was set free, traveled as far west as Spain, and years later was arrested again and put to death. It is just as likely, however, that he was not set

---

[15] This, it should be remembered, was not the same as Caesarea Philippi. See above, page 59.
[16] See Acts 25:10-12; 26:31-32.

free at all, but was killed, under Nero, at the same time that Peter was. Peter, not a Roman citizen, would have been crucified. According to tradition he felt unworthy to be treated like his Lord and was granted a request to be crucified upside down. Paul's death was more dignified.

The great, early struggle is reflected in nearly every letter from Paul's hand. It affected other parts of the New Testament too. It was, ultimately, the reason for Paul's imprisonment, and hence the reason why *Acts* was written. Some scholars think the controversy underlay the *Epistle to the Hebrews.*[17] A few think they see it also in *Revelation.* Almost certainly some of the Gospel source-materials were written while it was going on.[18]

In A.D. 62, however, James, who had become head of the Jerusalem Church, was martyred. After that the Jewish Christian Church came under heavy duress. Its followers were called *minim*, 'heretics,' by other Jews. Then in A.D. 70 came the destruction of Jerusalem, which was as harrowing to Christian Jews as to the others. The Christian Jews scattered northward from Jerusalem, and many of them settled in Pella, a town east of the Jordan. In A.D. 135 occurred the last Jewish rebellion against Rome, led by one Bar Kochba. During the struggle Christian Jews refused to call Bar Kochba 'Messiah,' and were the more despised and hounded by their compatriots.

The Jewish Christian Church continued for a few centuries. After A.D. 70, however, it was never again the Mother Church. Gradually its members separated into at

[17] St. Paul did not write Hebrews, and no one knows who did. Martin Luther suggested Apollos, which is not a bad guess. The personality which shines through Hebrews seems much like Apollos as described in Acts 18.
[18] See Pierson Parker, *The Gospel Before Mark* (University of Chicago Press, 1953).

least two groups. One remained fairly orthodox. The other not only denied important Christian beliefs, but went in for vegetarianism and other vagaries. Eventually the whole movement died out. To the end, its adherents called Paul an apostate or deserter from the Law. If only we knew more about these Jewish Christians! Perhaps they could tell us priceless things about the Man whom their fathers had known, and whom they and we have loved.

The decision of history went against those who would have made Christianity just another Jewish sect. The decision was right. Christianity was not just one more expression of Old Testament religion, but newer, more stupendous. Paul saw that, and in seeing he came close to Jesus' own view. Admittedly the Judaizers could cite, on their side, isolated words of Jesus. But they had to take them out of context. Nothing in the Gospels is plainer than that the disciples tried to put Jesus into a mold he did not fit. He burst the mold and, when Israel turned from him, he prophesied a new People of God under a new Law and Promise.

The decision of history was right. Yet we ought not glibly to call it right, without first seeing that there was much on the other side, and that strong men grieved over the outcome. Even their grief helped to fashion the New Testament faith.

THE FOURTH KEY:

TRUTH BY CONTRARIES

CHAPTER XV

THE WORLD UPSIDE DOWN

The New Testament is full of paradoxes. It habitually offers pairs of ideas which seem to contradict each other yet both of which, it says, are true. Earlier in this study we compared Christianity to the string of a bow: the string must be tugged in opposite directions or it would be no bow at all. Or it is like the shield under which two knights met. They disputed, then they fought, over whether the shield was black or white, when in fact it was black on one side and white on the other. Or it is like seeing the world with *two* eyes, so that objects come out into full, three-dimensional reality. (Three-dimensional motion pictures are a more startling instance of the same thing.) Whatever the analogy, there is in the New Testament religion a *principle of polarity* or, if you prefer, *contrariety*. The infinite and eternal Truth is too big for human words and human minds. When New Testament writers tried to state it, they had to speak in contraries. Without contraries they could not have spoken at all.

So the early Christians talked at times as if the New Age had already come, but at other times as though it were still in the offing. St. Paul reminded his readers that they had 'died' to sin—it had indeed been a real and exalting experience for them. Yet he warned them to be good, as though sin were still a live option to them—which it was.[1] St. Paul knew that while conversion always makes a difference, and usually a complete transformation, still the Christian has not lost his freedom to choose between right and wrong.

Presently we shall look at some further examples of this polarity with which the New Testament is replete. First, however, we must face a very real problem which the principle presents. It seems to say that in fact we never can comprehend the Christian religion, never get a consistent picture of it; that instead we must for ever be content with a bundle of contradictions. Almost instinctively our minds rebel against that. It is distressing to be told that the faith cannot be tied up in a neat package, with close-knit logic and no loose ends dangling. One may even be tempted to say that if Christianity is not really reasonable, it cannot really be true. Such a reaction would be quite understandable. Still, some comments can be made.

1. If Christianity offers data that are too big for our logic, there is nothing peculiar in that. The same thing happens in other fields. For instance, everybody in the world encounters gravity, and also electro-magnetism. Yet how long it was before these two could be covered in one mathematical equation—and even now, practically nobody understands the equation. Again, every one with eyes can enjoy a flower or a sunset; but few can reason about them scientifically and no one can do so perfectly. Or suppose a man refused to fall in love until he had a completely scientific and consistently logical understanding of her! Our facts outrun our intellects in every experience we have, at every level. Then what kind of God

[1] Above, pages 82f.; 118ff.

would He be if I could explain *Him*, with an intellect that cannot explain these other things?

2. The New Testament declares by its paradoxes that God does not weigh things in human scales. His estimate of what is true, and worthwhile, differs from man's. Long before Jesus was born, the unknown prophet of the Exile had said much the same thing:

> My thoughts are not your thoughts,
> Neither are your ways my ways,
>> Saith the Lord.
> For as the heavens are higher than the earth,
> So are my ways higher than your ways,
> And my thoughts than your thoughts. (*Isaiah* 55:8-9)

Man with his evil-doing contradicts God; but God, in this Gospel of His Son, this Christianity, contradicts man.

Certainly Christianity *ought* to be right at this point for, certainly, something is terribly askew in man's way of doing and thinking. Man resorts to force and politicking, to get the better of his fellow man. Rarely do these bring the satisfaction he had looked for and yet, as though knowing no other way, he keeps on using them. Man goes to war; and the aftermath, even in victory, is often worse than the evil he sought to destroy. Man masters the forces of nature, then cowers before the engines he has built. If God offered nothing better than that, He would be no God at all.

3. New Testament contrarieties correspond, furthermore, to a law of the universe. In physics we learn that 'for every action there is an equal and opposite reaction.' In ethics one hears of a 'law of compensation.' There is, likewise, a law of requital in religion. This world cannot remain for ever out of balance, with evil uncorrected, hopes unrealized and good unrewarded. Once more, God

would not be God if He could not, or would not, remedy all that. In the New Age toward which the New Testament thinkers looked, wrong must and will be righted. But that means, in turn, upsetting some cherished human notions. To really correct evil, really reward good, really satisfy the hope of mankind, the world must be turned topsy-turvy. New features, strange to the human mind, must be introduced into life. That is why, as St. Paul said, Christianity seems a stumblingblock to the Jews and foolishness to the Greeks (*I Corinthians* 1:18-25). To those, however, who make this faith their own, whether Jews or Greeks or any other, it is the power of God.

4. Finally, if our minds rebel at paradox, that is a very good thing. It means that we are goaded to seek for better and truer understanding. The Christian does not 'open his mouth and shut his eyes' to swallow whatever his religious leaders tell him. Quite the opposite, he must open his eyes. When he does, he beholds in this religion of deep mystery truths that are literally indescribable. (Karl Barth, an eminent Swiss theologian, once said that what American religion needs most is just this sense of mystery.) The Christian acknowledges these truths, because they are there. He will reason about them: he cannot help doing that. He will search, and ponder, and never shall he stop. Today he sees something. Tomorrow he may see further. Always, however, there will be more to learn and to think about. Always there will be the unfathomable beyond.

> Ah, but a man's reach should exceed his grasp,
> Or what's a heaven for?

Consider now some further examples of polarity in the New Testament. First we must look again at St. Paul. Certainly St. Paul had the sense of mystery. To none of

Jesus' followers, moreover, was the principle of truth-by-contraries more meaningful than to him. For there had been, in his earlier life, a contradiction that was no mere paradox, but shameful defeat:[2]

What shall we say then? Is the Law sin? No! Yet I had not known sin, except through the Law. When the commandment came, sin revived, and I died. The Law is spiritual, but I am carnal, sold under sin. For I do not practise what I would; but what I hate, that I do. To will is present with me, but to do that which is good is not. . . . (*Romans 7*)

The answer to this was a series of insights so gigantic that human syllogisms could not contain them. St. Paul saw that, although God is all-powerful, yet, in a way our minds do not fathom, He makes creatures able to resist His will. Paul did not resolve that paradox. Neither has any one since. We simply recognize the truth, that God is great enough to create responsible beings. We acknowledge, if we are honest with ourselves, that we are indeed responsible. That is as far as we can go.

Again St. Paul affirmed that God is loving and merciful, and yet he wrote of the 'wrath' of God. This wrath is no mere petulance or bad temper or frustrated anger. Quite the opposite, God is so infinitely good, and true and loving, that nothing ungodly—no evil, no lie, no hate, no pettiness—can continue in His presence. As darkness disappears when the light is lit, so surely and inescapably must evil vanish before Him. Thus the destruction of all that is ungodly in us is to be automatic, one might almost say impersonal. This is what other biblical writers meant when they warned, 'It is a fearful thing to fall into the hands of the living God.' 'Who may abide the day of his coming?' [3]

[2] Compare above, pages 114ff.
[3] Hebrews 10:31; Malachi 3:2.

So, in words which recall those of Jesus himself, St. Paul spoke of how God overthrows human ideas of value:[4]

Where is the wise? where is the scribe? where is the disputer of this world? Hath not God made foolish the wisdom of the world? For seeing that in the wisdom of God the world through its wisdom knew not God, it was God's good pleasure through the foolishness of the thing preached to save them that believe.

Not many wise after the flesh, not many mighty, not many noble [feel the call of Christ]. But God chose the foolish things of the world, that he might put to shame them that are wise; and God chose the weak things of the world, that he might put to shame the things that are strong; and the base things of the world, and the things that are despised, did God choose, yea and the things that are not, that he might bring to nought the things that are: that no flesh should glory before God; that, as it is written, he that glorieth, let him glory in the Lord.

We speak a wisdom not of this world: but we speak God's wisdom in a mystery. For who hath known the mind of the Lord that he should instruct him? But we have the mind of Christ.

The principle of contrariety, or polarity, affected Jesus' earlier followers too. It was, indeed, the reason that they did not at first understand their Master. When they did begin to understand, they themselves went out to 'turn the world upside down' as their opponents put it.

Says the author of the Epistle of James:

Hearken, my beloved brethren; did not God choose them that are poor as to the world to be rich in faith and heirs of the kingdom which he promised to them that love him? (*James 2:5*)

It was true. Few of Jesus' immediate followers came from the educated classes or the socially elite. 'I thank

[4] See I Corinthians 1:18-2:16. Compare Luke 10:21.

Thee, Heavenly Father,' Jesus prayed, 'that Thou hast hid this gospel from the wise and prudent, and hast revealed it unto babes.' [5] Publicans and harlots might get into the Kingdom ahead of the priests and rabbis, for the latter had been too self-assured or too perverse to repent when the chance came. To accept Jesus' own leadership meant such a reversal of values that one could no longer seek one's own advantage. 'Whosoever would be my disciple, let him deny himself and take up his cross and follow me.' [6] Yet self-denial would, if sincere, bring its own recompense:

Verily I say unto you, There is no man that hath left house, or brethren, or sisters, or mother, or father, or children, or lands, for my sake, and for the gospel's sake, but he shall receive a hundredfold now in this time, houses, and brethren, and sisters, and mothers, and children, and lands, with persecutions; and in the world to come eternal life. But many that are first shall be last: and the last first.[7]

His followers might appear few and poor now, but that too would be reversed. Jesus compared the situation to a grain of mustard seed. Tinier than the other seeds, it produces nonetheless a tree, in which the birds of the heaven may lodge.

Nor was the situation in which the disciples stood an accident. Rather, it was in line with the whole moral demand of God. The same paradox, the same upsetting of human values, comes out in Jesus' ethical teachings. What a topsy-turvy world it would be if everybody took these words seriously:

Whosoever would be first among you shall be your servant.

[5] See Matthew 11:25-30; Luke 10:21.
[6] Mark 8:34. Luke 9:23 reads, 'take up his cross daily.'
[7] Mark 10:23-31. No human offense was more hateful to Jesus than insincerity or hypocrisy. He condemned it again and again.

He that exalteth himself shall be abased, and he that humbleth himself shall be exalted.

The last shall be first and the first shall be last.

Blessed are the meek, for they shall inherit the earth.[8]

To Jesus, however, it was ordinary human life that was topsy-turvy, with outrageous injustice and man's inhumanity to man. The Reign of God is bound to turn such a world end for end, to redress wrongs, to brand as false what mankind too often takes to be true. Nearly every beatitude says that people, whom an untaught world might suppose to be in a sorry case, are *blessed*.[9] He enjoined his followers to 'love your *enemies*, do good to *those who hate you*.' Is this not the most contradictory of all his sayings? Can love be commanded? And if I love someone, is he still my enemy?

How absurd it is, said Jesus, to accumulate wealth on earth but fail to store up the really permanent treasure of heavenly things! Lazarus, who begs at the rich man's gate, may in the next life be blessed while the rich man has torment. 'What is a man profited, if he gain the whole world, and lose or forfeit his own self? What price will a man set on his own soul?' [10] In similar vein he said, 'How hard it is for those who trust in riches to enter the Kingdom! It is easier for a camel to go through the eye of a needle than for a rich man to enter the Kingdom of God.' That astonished the disciples. In the popular belief on which they had been raised, prosperity was a sign of God's approval, and poverty of His disapproval. 'Then

---

[8] See Matthew 5:5; 19:30; 20:16,26-27; 23:11-12; Mark 9:35; 10:31; Luke 13:30; 14:11; 18:14.

[9] This is true whether we take the more idealistic beatitudes of Matthew 5:3-12 or the more down-to-earth ones of Luke 6:21-26.

[10] Luke 9:25 = Mark 8:36-37; Luke 16:19-31. The latter is sometimes called the Parable of Dives and Lazarus. But *dives* is simply Latin for 'rich man.' It is not a name, and the man has none in Jesus' story.

who can be saved?' they asked. 'With God all things are possible,' Jesus answered. Despite his reply, people ever since have tried to explain his words away. It is sometimes said that he was talking about a gate called The Needle's Eye, so narrow that a camel could just squeeze through. That is bad archeology. Worse, it misses Jesus' sense of humor. He had a keen feeling for the ridiculous, and often used exaggeration. The full flavor of his words is, now and then, better brought out by a paraphrase:[11]

Which of you by worrying can add a foot to his height?

Can a blind man guide a blind man? Will they not both fall into a ditch?

When you give alms, do not blow a trumpet.

You Pharisees strain out a gnat and swallow a camel.

How can you say to your brother, 'Let me take the speck out of your eye,' and all the time you do not see the log in your own eye? Get rid of the log in your own eye, and then you can see clearly to remove the speck in your brother's eye.

How many readers of the Bible have, with long faces, missed the fun in Jesus' teaching! He poked fun because it is we mortals who are really paradoxical.

He was, however, in deadly earnest. 'He that saveth his life shall lose it, and he that loseth his life shall find it.' No words of Jesus are better attested than these. They are quoted, with but slight variation, five times, in passages representing nearly every source underlying the Gospels: *Matthew* 16:25; *Mark* 8:35; *Luke* 9:24; 17:33; *John* 12:25. And none more nearly sum up the meaning and course of his own ministry. This brings us to the high point in

---

[11] See Matthew 6:27; Luke 6:39; Matthew 6:2; 23:24; 7:3-5. 'Foot,' in the first saying here, is literally 'cubit,' about 19 inches.

New Testament polarity. Polarity underlay Jesus' own life, and his thoughts concerning himself.

It is seen at his baptism. Huge crowds had gone out to hear John the Baptist. Jesus went too, and was baptized. Here it is well to digress a moment, to see what this baptism was. The rite was an ancient Jewish one, but with meanings often different from those of Christian baptism. The Jews did baptize proselytes (i.e., converts to their religion), but they also used the ceremony for other purposes: to release one from a religious vow; to show that one was rid of a loathsome disease; or, as under John the Baptist, to mark a great religious awakening. Conceivably one might be baptized several times. Most early Christians seem to have thought John's baptism sufficient for Church membership. The disciples, like Jesus, were baptized by John,[12] and there is no record of their repeating the rite. Similarly Apollos, a convert from John's movement, was not baptized a second time. On the other hand St. Paul did rebaptize some people who came over from John's group.[13] Perhaps this is one more area where the apostles disagreed and the Church had to work out a decision. Whatever the early Christians thought of John's rite, they seem to have been unanimous that baptism itself is an essential step in initiation to Christianity.

As Jesus came up from the water, he saw a vision and heard a voice. Some of the Gospels imply that the bystanders saw and heard too; but Mark, the earliest of the Four, says that Jesus had the experience alone.[14] Far more important than these differences are the words which he heard:

---

[12] That is, at least, the implication of passages like Acts 1:21-22; John 1:35-42; Matthew 21:23-32.

[13] See Acts 18:24-28; 19:1-6.

[14] Luke 3:21-22; John 1:32-34; Mark 1:9-11.

Thou art My Son:
My Beloved in whom I am well pleased.

While some English Bibles print the words in a slightly different order, this arrangement is correct. The first line is from *Psalm 2, a hymn in honor of the Messiah*. The second line is from *Isaiah 42, a poem on the Suffering Servant*. Thus at the threshold of his ministry there came together in Jesus' mind these two figures from his nation's noblest thinking. Except for the name of God, no words in Israel's language were more exalted or freighted with meaning.

But now notice. *These two terms*, Messiah and Suffering Servant, *are opposed to each other*. The Suffering Servant lacked beauty, was tormented, bruised, buffeted about, despised—the words recall Israel at her own lowest ebb of fortune. Messiah, in contrast, was the Anointed One of the Lord, Prince, King, Victor, high and mighty Potentate—heap on him all the grand epithets you will, you cannot exhaust what the Jews expected from his coming. In fact Messiah, as they thought of him, was coming specifically to erase the marks of the Suffering Servant! So huge and obvious were the differences between the two figures that almost nobody had thought to connect them. True, one or two writers had suggested that one or two poems in *Isaiah 40-66* might refer to the Messiah. They did not develop the idea, however, nor did it influence the thinking of their contemporaries. To most Jews the suggestion that Messiah might suffer would have been grossly offensive. That he should die was unthinkable.

'We preach Christ crucified, unto the Jews a stumbling-block,' said St. Paul; and preachers today talk about 'the scandal of the Cross.' Are we shocked by the scandal? or

have we heard about it too often? Think what Christianity was saying to the Jews:

Your Messiah, the One for whom your people have waited
these many centuries, has indeed come. But he has been
abused and humiliated by common, unclean Roman soldiers.
He has been led about the streets for all to see, and then
executed, along with two robbers, as a felon. Before his
execution, the Christians went on to say, the whipped and
sorry figure was made to stand before a Jewish crowd, and
Pilate jeered, 'Behold, your king!'

Can we feel the revulsion, the sickening shame, that
would engulf a loyal first-century Jew? The tale was so
damnable that, in city after city, devout Jews did their
best to stamp Christianity out.

They could not. For nineteen centuries the contradiction of his life has been told in song and story. He is worshipped by the world's most rich and powerful: Yet he
was born in a stable and brought up, most likely, in a
one-room house with a dirt floor. His description of a
woman who swept the floor for a lost coin and, when she
found it, excitedly told the neighbors, is probably a picture of his own mother (*Luke 15:8-10*). Today his name
is better known than any other in ancient history: In his
own time, however, he was so obscure that historians
hardly noticed him. Their notes are enough to prove that
he existed, but no more, and John the Baptist was much
more famous. At Christmas we hear Luke's song about
the 'Savior who is Christ the Lord': Jesus, however, joined
the peasants and the delinquents in submitting to John's
baptism. Jesus' words and doings have inspired more
books than has any other subject in the world: Yet he
himself left not a line of writing. The creeds depict him
reigning at the right hand of God; and he is called 'Chris-
tus Victor': Yet his defeat was so complete that in the

end he cried, *My God, my God, why hast Thou forsaken me?* [15]

He saw the contradiction. He embraced it. Most important of all, he made it the basis of his own claim. Peter might call him Messiah, and James and John seek thrones alongside his in the coming Kingdom. Yet 'the foxes have holes and the birds of the air have their nests, but the son of man hath not where to lay his head.' With supreme but no doubt unconscious irony, those who knew him best and stood to profit most directly and intensely from him turned against him. His relatives and acquaintances did it in Nazareth. His disciples did it in Gethsemane.

> He came to his own things,
> And his own people received him not.

Several strands of tradition record Jesus' reply: 'A prophet is not without honor save in his own country and among his own kin and in his own house.' [16]

Out of the brilliance of Jesus' own teaching and Jesus' own life comes this polarity, this contrariety. It is no blind and self-disproving contradiction. It is the two ends of the taut bow-string. It is the two eyes that we must have to see clearly. It is, for those who are willing, a light to lighten every page of the New Testament. For if 'the son of man came not to be served but to serve, and to give his life a ransom for many,' nevertheless, 'ye call me Master and Lord, and ye say well, for so I am.' [17]

---

[15] Mark 15:34. The words are the first line of Psalm 22. Other lines in the Psalm are astonishingly like events of Jesus' crucifixion, and were undoubtedly running through his mind as he hung on the cross. That the line is from a Psalm does not reduce in the slightest his sense of devastation as he spoke it.

[16] Mark 6:4; Luke 4:24; John 4:44. See further Luke 4:16-30; 9:58; Mark 3:21; 14:50; John 1:11.

[17] Mark 10:45; John 13:13.

CHAPTER XVI

THE KINGDOM OF GOD

When Jesus began his ministry in Galilee, his preaching was at first identical with John the Baptist's: 'Repent, for the Kingdom of God [or Kingdom of Heaven] is at hand' (*Matthew 3:1-2; 4:12,17*). After that, although his work diverged more and more from John's, Jesus kept on talking about the Kingdom.

The expressions 'Kingdom of God' and 'Kingdom of Heaven' are interchangeable. Matthew usually reads 'Heaven.' This was preferred by Jewish Christians who, like other Jews, felt that the name of God was too sacred to repeat constantly. The other Gospels nearly always have 'Kingdom of God.' The latter is more explicit, of course, and has been more popular in the Gentile Church. Jesus evidently used both forms, though as a Jew he may have said 'Kingdom of Heaven' more often.

Now, however, we meet a strange situation. Jesus had more to say about the Kingdom than about almost anything else. Yet Christians, the world over, have not agreed as to what he meant by it. In fact, no less than seven possibilities have been suggested!

(1) 'Kingdom' means, literally, 'rule' or 'reign.' That is true not only in English but in Greek, the language of the New Testament; and also in Aramaic, the language Jesus spoke. Furthermore Jesus said, 'The Kingdom of

God is within you.'[1] Therefore the Kingdom of God, as he thought of it, is a spiritual experience of God's rule in our individual lives.

(2) A kingdom is a social structure, a community of people. Both Jesus and his apostles did in fact proclaim a new people or new Israel. This was the community of Christians; that is, it was the Church. 'Kingdom of God' means the Church. (Should we include, also, the fellowship of Christians who have passed on to the next life?)

(3) While 'Kingdom' implies social structure, 'of God' means 'as God would have it.' Therefore 'Kingdom of God' means society arranged in accordance with the will of God or, to use a once popular phrase, it is 'the ideal social order.'

(4) Both Jesus and the apostles envisaged a new era. Perhaps they thought it had already begun, but certainly it was not complete. Jesus asked his disciples to pray, 'May Thy Kingdom come.' Hence 'Kingdom of God' refers to the New Age which the apocalyptists foresaw, when God will come to 'turn and overturn' and establish, say in the New Jerusalem, His throne.

(5) God's throne is in heaven. Only in heaven will life go on for ever, so only there can God's rule be permanent. Hence 'Kingdom of God' or 'Kingdom of Heaven' means the place where good people go when they die.

(6) Like John the Baptist, Jesus warned his hearers to *repent* ere the Kingdom come. So 'Kingdom of God' must mean the final Judgment—approximately what St. Paul meant by 'the wrath of God.'

(7) Or should we come more into line with popular Jewish ideas of the time? The precise expressions 'Kingdom of God' and 'Kingdom of Heaven' had not been used much; but phrases like 'His Kingdom,' 'Thy Kingdom,'

[1] Luke 17:21; but on the meaning of the saying see below, page 161f.

· *159*

'the kingdom shall be the Lord's' are frequent in contemporary literature. Nearly every Jew who heard Jesus' phrase would think of *Israel:* Israel restored to freedom and established as the leader of the world. At the Triumphal Entry the disciples themselves shouted about 'the kingdom of our father David' and Jesus did not stop them. Even after the Resurrection they asked, 'Wilt thou at this time restore the kingdom to Israel?'—and Jesus' only reply was, 'It is not for you to know the times which the Father hath set within his own authority.'[2] Therefore 'Kingdom of God' meant nothing else than the restoration of Israel.

Whatever choice we make from this array, we shall find ourselves agreeing with some of the keenest minds in Christendom. Is it not a sorry spectacle that, with all Jesus' discussion, Christians cannot make up their minds what he was driving at?

One reason for the difficulty lies, of course, in our own dispositions. We are prone to read into the Bible ideas that we want to find there.[3] For example, statement (1), above, appeals to those who emphasize piety, or divine guidance in their personal affairs. People who think of religion as mostly moral behavior like it too. Statement (2) is often put forward by those of a Catholic bent. Statement (3) was popular in the early decades of the twentieth century, when social reform was in the air. Adventists, who long for Christ to come and put an end to this unhappy world, are likely to prefer statement (4).

There is, however, another reason for differences of interpretation. Notice that statements (1), (2), and (3) all describe the Kingdom as something to be realized

[2] Mark 11:7-10; Acts 1:3-8. See also Luke 19:39-40; Matthew 21:15-16.
[3] Compare above, pages 14-15.

here and now. It is already present, potentially at least, and it may even be inward and invisible. In contrast, statements (4) through (7) envisage the Kingdom as *in the future.* Now this division corresponds to a real division in Jesus' own teachings. He said things about the Kingdom which seem at first to contradict each other. In fact this is one of the most striking cases of polarity in the whole New Testament.

On the one hand, Jesus insisted that the Kingdom is present now, even that it is spiritual and inward. Some Pharisees once asked him when the Kingdom of God would come (*Luke 17:20ff*). He answered, 'The Kingdom of God cometh not with observation, neither shall men say, "Lo, here," or, "There." For behold, the Kingdom of God is within you.' The word here translated 'within' is Greek *entós* which could mean 'among' instead—'The Kingdom is in your midst.' While some translators prefer the latter, 'within' is much more likely. Had St. Luke meant to imply 'among' there were other expressions which he could and usually did use; whereas in the only other occurrence of *entós* in the New Testament, it plainly means 'inside of.' [4] Whether Jesus meant that the Kingdom was 'within you' or 'in your midst,' however, in either case he was telling these Pharisees that it was already present, there and then. On another occasion he said, 'If I by the Spirit [Luke reads "finger"] of God cast out demons, then the Kingdom of God has come upon you.' 'Heal the sick,' he charged his disciples, 'and say to them, "The Kingdom of God has come upon you." ' His parables nearly always speak of the Kingdom in the present tense: 'The Kingdom of God is like. . . .' 'So is the Kingdom of God, as if. . . .' To a scribe who had de-

[4] 'That which is within the cup,' Matthew 23:26.

clared that love is the fulfilling of the Law, Jesus replied, 'Thou art not far from the Kingdom of God.'[5] Jesus' thought along these lines was reflected by St. Paul, who wrote, 'The Kingdom of God is not eating and drinking, but righteousness and peace and joy in the Holy Spirit.'[6]

Yet with equal certainty Jesus treated the Kingdom as an external, objective event of the future. He began his work with the announcement, 'The Kingdom of God has come near.' He said, 'They *shall see* the son of man come in his Kingdom.' 'Then the righteous *shall shine* forth as the sun in the Kingdom of their Father.'[7] And while his parables of the Kingdom sometimes use the present tense, others speak of the future, and even more urgently. A fish-net draws up all kinds, but the fisherman throws the bad away; so in the Kingdom, the workers of lawlessness will be cast out. Weeds may be growing among the wheat now, but at the harvest the weeds will be separated out and burned—and the Kingdom is like that. Precisely because it is a hope of the future, his disciples are told to pray, 'Thy kingdom come.'

The mistake is to seize one part of the truth, when both parts are true. The Kingdom is for ever inward yet for ever outward. It is for ever present yet for ever coming. Only when both truths take hold in our minds shall we find the tensile strength that the Kingdom has to impart.

However, Jesus did not leave his followers to wrestle unaided with a collection of paradoxes. He said other things about the Kingdom. These bring the seeming contradictions into unity, and raise his concept high.

[5] See Matthew 12:28 = Luke 11:20; Luke 10:9; Mark 12:34. The chief parables of the Kingdom are in Matthew 13 and Mark 4.
[6] Romans 14:17. St. Paul spoke frequently of the inward, moral nature of the Kingdom; see I Corinthians 4:20; 6:9; 15:50; Galatians 5:21; Colossians 1:13-14; I Thessalonians 2:10-12.
[7] Mark 1:14-15; Matthew 16:27-28; 13:43.

Note, first, that it is a *Kingdom*. The word is not widely familiar today, and its unfamiliarity may lead us into 'the peril of modernizing Jesus.' If the word makes us think of a limited monarchy (like those of England or Sweden, for instance), or of modern social reform, or of nineteenth-century religious individualism, in each case we shall be a far cry from the way first-century people thought. True, Jesus towered above his time. Yet, once more, he had to communicate his message in the words and traditions that people around him knew. We have seen how he did, in fact, express himself in first century terms, expanding them, certainly, but not throwing them away. In first-century language, then, 'kingdom' meant a social structure, a corporate community, *a people under a king*. That meaning lay behind Jesus' phrase.

One series of events, in particular, should deepen our understanding of Jesus' intent. At the Last Supper he once more spoke of the Kingdom as a thing still to come: 'I will no more drink of the fruit of the vine until I drink it anew with you in my Father's kingdom.' On the cross he grew thirsty but would not drink. Yet, said the Apostles soon afterward, 'We ate and drank with him after he was raised from the dead.' [8] That is, he had refused to drink until the Kingdom came, but he did drink in the fellowship of the young Church. The connection cannot be accidental. Part of the truth—if only a part—is that the Kingdom of God comprises His faithful people, His beloved community, His Church. To be Christian is to say, 'We . . . our . . . us,' '*Our* Father, thine is the kingdom.'

[8] Matthew 26:29 = Mark 14:25; Mark 15:23; Acts 10:40-42. Is it hard to believe in Jesus' physical resurrection? At the moment that does not matter, since we are concerned only with what the early Christians believed. Clearly they did think Jesus rose physically from the dead. The subject is discussed below, Chapter XXII.

Second, the Kingdom is not man-made. It is *of God*. Some modern writers (and even some preachers who should know better) speak of 'building the Kingdom of God'; or they picture it coming gradually, perhaps as the outcome of social evolution. Such ideas were typical of the nineteenth century; but they are foreign to Jesus' teaching, as they are to the entire New Testament. On one occasion Jesus did compare the Kingdom to a seed which a man plants (*Mark 4:26-29*). However, the emphasis of the parable is not on growth. It is on mystery:

The Kingdom is as if . . . the seed should spring up and grow, *he knoweth not how*.

Man knows not how, for it is given of God. Man is to search for the Kingdom, and make ready to enter it. He must be prepared if need be to give up everything for it, even his eye or his hand or his last earthly possession.[9] But the Kingdom comes from God alone. In the ancient Latin phrase it is a *mysterium, tremendum et luminosum*.

The parable of the seed, just mentioned, illustrates a law that must be applied to all Jesus' stories: A parable normally teaches just one lesson. It should be used only for the main lesson it emphasizes. If this rule is ignored the results will sometimes be startling. For example:

There was in a city a judge, who feared not God and regarded not man. And there was a widow. And she came oft unto him, saying, Avenge me of mine adversary. And he would not for a while: but afterward he said, Because this widow troubleth me, I will avenge her, lest she wear me out by her continual coming.

This teaches the value of persistent prayer. Do not deduce from it that God is unfair, or that He gets worn out! Again,

[9] Matthew 5:29-30; 13:44-46; Mark 10:21.

The kingdom of heaven is like unto a treasure hidden in the field; which a man found, and hid; and in his joy he goeth and selleth all that he hath, and buyeth that field.

This teaches that the Kingdom is unspeakably valuable. Do not deduce that we should cheat in our purchases.[10]

Finally, all the past and future of the Kingdom, its inwardness and outwardness, its spiritual and visible aspects, are brought together and made one by Jesus' personal claim. *The Kingdom is all these things because its King is all these things.* Presently we shall have more to say about Jesus' claim, but listen now to his final parable about this Kingdom:

When the son of man shall come in his glory, then shall he sit upon the throne of his glory: and before him shall be gathered all nations. Then shall the King say unto them on his right hand, Come, ye blessed of my Father, inherit the kingdom prepared for you from the foundation of the world. (*Matthew 25:31-46*)

His words are the sanction for a prayer which many use today. Indeed some people say it, or listen to it, every day of their lives:

> *Almighty and everliving God, we most heartily thank thee, that we are very members incorporate in the mystical body of thy Son, which is the blessed company of all faithful people; and are also heirs through hope of thy everlasting kingdom. And we humbly beseech thee, O heavenly Father, so to assist us with thy grace, that we may continue in that holy fellowship; through Jesus Christ our Lord.*[11]

[10] Luke 18:1-7; Matthew 13:44.
[11] From the Post-Communion Thanksgiving (adapted), The Book of Common Prayer.

CHAPTER XVII

THE SON OF MAN

As Jesus and his disciples walked along the road near Caesarea Philippi, he asked them, 'Who do men say that I am?' 'Some say that you are a prophet,' they replied. 'Some believe that you are one of the ancient prophets come back to life—Jeremiah perhaps, or Elijah. Herod is afraid you are John the Baptist.' In those days, you will recall, it was a common notion that deceased heroes might return at times of great moment.[1]

'But who do *you* believe that I am?' Jesus asked. Then Simon, that changeable and impetuous man, made his great reply. He was the one who later would swear that he did not know Jesus. Still later he would vacillate over the question of carrying Christianity to the Gentiles, until St. Paul got quite exasperated with him. Yet on this same journey to Caesarea Philippi Jesus would dub him 'Peter' or 'Rock.' For he also was the one who, at the start of Jesus' ministry, had caught a glimpse of Jesus' meaning and had cried, 'Depart from me, for I am a sinful man, O Lord!' Again, after the Resurrection, it would be Simon Peter who would conquer his terror, and summon the Jewish leaders themselves: 'Let all the house of Israel understand beyond a doubt that God hath made him

[1] Matthew 16:13-20; Mark 8:27-30. See page 73 above.

both Lord and Messiah, this Jesus whom ye crucified.'
(*Acts 2:36*)

'Thou art the Messiah,' said Simon; or, as *Matthew* has
it, 'Thou art the Messiah, the Son of the living God.'

There is a remarkable parallel between the account of
Peter's confession and the story, which comes just before
it in *Mark*, about a blind man:

Mark 8:22-26	*Mark 8:27-29*
And he took hold of the blind man by the hand and brought him out of the village; and when he had spit on his eyes and laid his hands upon him, he asked him,	And Jesus went forth and his disciples into the villages of Caesarea Philippi; and in the way he asked his disciples, saying unto them, Who do men say that I am?
Seest thou anything? And he looked up, and said, I see men as trees, walking.	And they told him, saying, John the Baptist; and others, Elijah; but others, one of the prophets.
Then again he laid his hands upon his eyes; and he looked steadfastly, and was restored, and saw all things clearly. And he sent him away to his home, saying, Tell it to no one in the village.	And he asked them, But who say ye that I am? Peter answereth and saith unto him, Thou art the Christ. And he charged them that they should tell no man of him.

This pairing might be a coincidence. More likely the
Gospel author put it this way—or did Jesus himself deliberately plan it?—so as to underscore the momentous
import of Peter's words. The people, even the disciples,
had been blind and slow to perceive. Now the disciples
saw clearly.

With Peter's confession the story in the Gospels turns a
corner. It is an actual, physical turning, for Jesus at once
started back southward to go to Jerusalem. It is a spiritual
turning too. At Jerusalem death was waiting. The black

and angular shadow of the cross fell athwart Jesus' mind as he tried to show the disciples what Peter's reply really meant. 'The son of man will be handed over to foreigners,' he warned. 'He will be spit on, whipped, and then killed.' [2] Today we know the story too well. Only by strong effort of the imagination can we sense the shock that overtook these men when their glad acclaim was changed into this revolting augury. 'No, no!' said Peter. 'Far be it from thee, Lord. This shall not happen to thee!' 'Get thee behind me, Satan! Thou mindest not the things that are of God, but the things that are of men.'

So they turned south. The Gospels picture the group: Jesus stalking grimly ahead; his friends following along, not knowing what else to do, but at a distance, reluctant, muttering among themselves. The gathering gloom brought again a stern and sombre note into Jesus' preaching. Earlier in his ministry he, like John the Baptist, had told of a God who comes in judgment and who demands a decision. This teaching had not been prominent during most of his Galilean activities, but now it was heard again. A man came to him and said, 'I will follow thee, but first let me go and wind up some business affairs.' Jesus answered, 'No man putting his hand to the plough and looking back is fit for the Kingdom of God.' Another said, 'I will follow thee, but first let me go and bury my father.' Jesus replied, 'Let the dead bury their dead! Go thou and preach the Kingdom of God.' He said, 'He that is not against us is for us'; and again, 'He that is not with me is against me, and he that gathereth not with me scattereth.' [3] There is no middle ground. You are on one side or you are on the other. Thus Jesus echoed what

[2] Matthew 16:21-23; Mark 9:31; 10:33-34.
[3] Luke 9:59-62; Mark 9:38-40; Matthew 12:38.

Joshua had said of old, 'Choose you this day whom ye will serve.' [4]

It was during this period that Jesus made the greatest use of the expression *son of man*. 'Let these words sink unto your ears: the Son of man shall be delivered up into the hands of men.' (*Luke 9:44*) In designating himself thus, what did Jesus mean to imply? 'Son of man,' like 'Kingdom of God,' has been the subject of much debate. The phrase sounds odd to us, as it did to the earliest Greek-speaking Christians, because neither they nor we are used to the idiom. In fact they found Jesus' title so enigmatic and mysterious that they hardly ever used it except in writing the Gospels. This, incidentally, is a sign of the basic trustworthiness of these New Testament books. *They put on Jesus' lips a term which the Church could not and would not have invented for its own use.*

However, the Jews of Palestine *were* in the habit of speaking of 'the son of' something. 'Son of this-or-that' meant one who partakes of this-or-that nature. A man with prophetic gifts would be called 'son of a prophet.' One who was prodigiously evil was a 'son of Belial'; and so on. Thus 'son of man' meant 'a human being,' 'one who is truly a man.' The psalms frequently use the phrase in this way, as a poetic equivalent for 'man.' Probably the best-known example is,[5]

> What is man that thou art mindful of him,
> Or the son of man that thou visitest him?

[4] Joshua 24:15. Notice, by the way, that *Jesus* and *Joshua* are two forms of the same name. In Hebrew it means, 'The Lord is my salvation,' and that is why at Matthew 1:21 we read, 'Thou shalt call his name JESUS; for it is he that shall *save* his people. . . .' At Acts 7:45 and Hebrews 4:8 some English Bibles have 'Jesus' where the Joshua of the Old Testament is meant.

[5] Psalm 8:4. See also Psalms 80:17; 144:3; 146:3.

Jesus actually quoted the psalm from which these lines come. There can be no doubt that, in using the phrase 'son of man,' he was moved by its constant use in the Old Testament. Then the term would underscore his human character. He is 'the Man' or 'the Person.'

But that itself sounds like a claim of some sort. So we must still ask, What kind of claim? Now there are two ancient books in which *the Messiah* is pictured as a 'son of man.' In the 7th chapter of *Daniel* the author describes a series of creatures that he saw in a dream: a lion, a bear, a leopard, a horned beast, and finally 'one like unto a son of man,' i.e., 'a figure in human form.' Each of these creatures represents a nation. The last, the human figure, is Israel. It is Israel, however, itself acting like a Messiah to the world.

Then there is a book called the *Similitudes of Enoch*, named, like so many apocalypses, for an Old Testament hero. This book is regarded as Scripture by the Abyssinian Church, though not by Christians in the West. It was known to the author of *Jude* and perhaps to one or two other New Testament writers. Jesus may have been acquainted with it. In it the Messiah is described as 'a son of man.' The phrase is no more a title here than it is in *Daniel* or *Psalms*. It simply pictures the Messiah as having a human shape. Still, it may be that by Jesus' time the words had got associated, in people's minds, with these descriptions of the Messiah. In that case, when Jesus called himself 'son of man' the words would suggest to his hearers that he claimed to be the Anointed One. This seems the more likely when we recall that Jesus rarely used the term until after Peter's confession. When he did use it, furthermore, it was sometimes while describing the glory of his coming reign:[6]

[6] Matthew 25:31; Mark 13:26; Matthew 19:28. Other examples are at Matthew 16:27-28; Mark 8:38; 13:32; 14:62; Luke 12:40; 17:24.

When the son of man shall come in his glory, and all the angels with him, then shall he sit on the throne of his glory.

Then shall they see the son of man coming in clouds with great power and glory.

When the son of man shall sit on the throne of his glory . . .

Yet such passages are relatively few. Most of the time, when Jesus called himself 'son of man,' he was talking not about his future eminence but about his *suffering:*[7]

The foxes have holes, and the birds of the heaven have nests; but the son of man hath not where to lay his head.

We go up to Jerusalem; and the son of man shall be delivered unto the chief priests and scribes; and they shall condemn him to death.

The son of man must suffer many things, and be rejected, and be killed.

The son of man is delivered up into the hands of men, and they shall kill him; and when he is killed, after three days he shall rise again.

The son of man came not to be ministered unto but to minister, and to give his life a ransom for many.

The hour is come; behold, the son of man is betrayed into the hands of sinners.

Judas, betrayest thou the son of man with a kiss?

Here is no victorious Messiah. Here is a suffering servant of the Lord! So we look again at the Old Testament. And it is supremely interesting to discover that 'son of man' is used by the very prophet who wrote about the Servant. Once the prophet represents God as saying,[8]

[7] Matthew 8:20; 20:18; Mark 8:31; 9:31; 10:45; 14:41; Luke 22:48. See also Matthew 12:40; 17:12; 26:2; Mark 10:33; Luke 6:22; 24:7. Compare John 3:14; 8:28.
[8] Isaiah 51:12-13; 56:1-2.

I, even I, am he that comforteth you:
Who art thou, that thou shouldst be afraid
   of a man that shall die
      and of *the son of man* which shall be made as grass;
And forgettest the Lord thy Maker?

Again,

Thus saith the Lord,
My salvation is near to come,
And my righteousness to be revealed.
Blessed is the man that doeth this,
And *the son of man* that layeth hold upon it.

As with *Psalm 8*, the last lines are from a poem part of which Jesus himself quoted. In each of these passages 'son of man' is a mere equivalent for 'man' and, in the context, cannot mean anything else. Here, however, is a 'son of man' who will grasp the righteousness and salvation of God, will do His will and, in the first passage, will die. Moreover both passages follow closely upon poems about the Servant of the Lord. It would have been completely natural, therefore, when Jesus used the title 'son of man,' for him and his hearers to remember the prophet's words and to think of the Suffering Servant.

Now notice another group of Jesus' sayings:[9]

It is written of the son of man, that he should suffer many things and be set at nought.

The son of man goeth, even as *it is written* of him: but woe unto that man through whom the son of man is betrayed!

All the things that are written by the prophets shall be accomplished unto the son of man. For he shall be delivered up unto the Gentiles, and shall be mocked, and shamefully treated, and spit upon: and they shall scourge and kill him . . .

[9] Mark 9:12-13; 14:21; Luke 18:31-32. Also Luke 22:37; 24:46. The solemn introduction, 'It is written,' means, It stands in the Word of God and has the warrant of eternal truth.

Those things had never been written of the Messiah! A scourged and dishonored Messiah was farthest from Jewish thinking. Jesus' words, here, describe no one else than the Suffering Servant whom the ancient seer had envisaged, who should by his pain bear the sins of the world. Indeed, says St. Luke, Jesus quoted that prophet again: 'I say unto you, that this which is written must be fulfilled in me, "And he was reckoned with transgressors." For that which concerneth me hath fulfilment.'

Thus Jesus' title carries the same fusing of two great ideas as we found in the Voice at his baptism. The Son of Man is reckoned with transgressors, a man of sorrows and acquainted with grief. He is also Judge of the world. He is King over all kings; but he is betrayed by his friends and jeered at by strangers. The Son of Man is the Messiah, and he is the Suffering Servant of God.

Once more do we feel the gripping paradox of the Christ? Perhaps we are ready now to pray, as Christians long have prayed,

Almighty God, whose most dear Son went not up to joy but first he suffered pain, and entered not into glory before he was crucified; Mercifully grant that we, walking in the way of the cross, may find it none other than the way of life and peace; through the same thy Son Jesus Christ our Lord.

THE FIFTH KEY:

PHYSICAL AND SPIRITUAL

CHAPTER XVIII

THE WHOLE CREATION

While we have said much about dilemmas and para-doxes, there is one that we have not discussed. To many it may seem the most common, and at the same time, most difficult of all. Philosophers have written hundreds of books about it. Every religion has wrestled with it. Every person has faced it, consciously or unconsciously; and the course of a man's life will be fixed very largely by what attitude he takes to it. The dilemma has many names. It may be called the conflict between spirit and body; or between mind and matter; or between the visible world and the invisible.

On the one hand there is physique. How much of a person's time is devoted to his own body, feeding, cleans-ing, clothing, resting, repairing it, giving it pleasure? or in doing such things for other people's bodies? or getting ready to do them, or earning the means to do them? In the course of all this activity, how many material objects must he handle or look at? In reacting to other people, are we affected by their physical appearance and physical behavior? Do we gauge our own or another's success by income, or by how often one's name appears in print? Does it appear that life is just *matter* and nothing else?

If we decide that the answer is 'Yes,' however, see what happens! Let a man surrender to physique, allow a con-

cern for material things to dominate his life, and he is
cheated. Life becomes stunted or bitter or frantic or
meaningless, and he is on the toboggan. This truth is so
well known that it is almost hackneyed. 'The best things
in life are free.' Yes, and they are invisible: truth, loyalty,
friendship, unselfishness, serenity. How many stories are
written about poor persons who found those things, or
about wealthy ones who did not! Even if a man neglects
them in himself, he will nearly always prize them when
he meets them in other people. Every one, who tells himself the truth, knows in his heart that there is an invisible
world of divine things, and that he belongs in that world.
As St. Augustine put it, 'O God, Thou hast made us for
Thyself; and our hearts shall never rest until they rest
in Thee.'

Thus man's nature has about it much that is material,
but much that is spiritual, too. He has, or is, both a body
and a soul. Then what is the real connection between
these two parts of him? Every religion and every philosophy of life can be classified according to the way in
which it answers that question.

1. There are those who say that matter, and physical
events, are all that really exist. So-called 'spiritual' things
are like the waves of the sea: they are shapes or activities
that come and go on the surface of a material universe,
but have no separate existence of their own. Is it strange
to call such a point of view religious? It has nevertheless
found religious expression. For instance, the most primitive form of religion is *animism*. This regards physical
objects, like trees, streams or hills, as themselves gods to
be propitiated. Distinguish carefully between animism
and *animatism*. The latter does believe in an invisible
spirit world: the tree or river is not itself a god, but is
occupied or *animated* by a god. When primitive man

moved from animism to animatism, it was one of the greatest forward strides that religion ever took.

Another and very different example is dialectical materialism, whose most familiar representative is Communism. This bids us find satisfaction in material processes alone. As many people have recognized, Communism has the earmarks of a living religion: an authoritative literature or 'bible,' a careful and close-knit organization, vigilant rooting out of unorthodox opinions, and missionary activity and the zeal to make converts.

The idea, that physique is all that counts, finds also more subtle religious forms. One movement, widely known today, is called 'Christian Naturalism.' This gives new twists to Christian words, so as to make them fit a materialistic world view. For example, 'God' means whatever you find most worthwhile in the universe, such as the process of coöperation or integration. 'Judgment' means that we must either join with others in mutual service, or reap the consequences of not doing so. 'Prayer' means turning our minds toward the best. 'Immortality' means our influence on those who live after us; and so on.

Then there is Humanism, which is considerably older. Humanism says that human life, here and now, is the highest good there is. In the United States many public schools, in effect, teach Humanism, in their refusal to teach any form of religion.

Most insidious of all is the social culture in which all of us live. This culture leads us, often, to judge life by purely materialistic standards. Much of the time, our society either ignores spiritual religion altogether, or else condescendingly allows it a minor place. Even the phrase 'standard of living' refers almost exclusively to physical possessions! With matter and spirit competing for his allegiance, western man is under constant pressure to put his faith in matter, and let the spirit go.

2. In sharp contrast are some religions of the Orient, notably Hinduism and Buddhism. For these, the world of physical happenings is *maya* (pronounce 'mah'yah') or illusion. Reality is like a pane of glass. If the glass were perfect it would be invisible; but a crack or imperfection in it can be seen. Whatever we can see or touch, the physical world, is like the crack in the glass. It is no part of the glass. It is evil and has no right to be there. I am caught in this world, in a continuous round of reincarnations. In successive lives I shall have good or ill fortune, and shall be a human or an animal—or a woman!—depending on what I have earned in previous incarnations. My aim, then, is to escape entirely from this material world and be absorbed into Nirvana or the Absolute. (The great claim of Buddhism is that, unlike Hinduism, it offers a definite plan of escape.) Thus the *real* world has no part with matter and history. Physical things and physical occurrences are evil, illusory, and despised. So effective was this teaching that the people of India kept no records of passing events, and it is almost impossible now to write a history of their land.

Facing the tension between spirit and matter, these Orientals put their faith in spirit and let matter go. This way out has also attracted many westerners. Essentially it is what metaphysical idealism has said: Ultimate reality is mental or spiritual, and physical events are only the ideas of spirit or mind.[1] Greek religion sometimes expressed a similar notion. More significant for us, there have been many efforts to make Christianity, likewise, deny that matter and history are true:

[1] See above, pages 15f.

(a) Many early Christians were affected by a religious movement called *Gnosticism*. The word is from Greek *gnosis,* 'knowledge.' The basic idea behind Gnosticism was that the All-perfect One can have no contact with our imperfect, limited, material world. Between the two there are various intermediate stages of being. Each stage emanates or flows out of the one next above it. Some Greeks personified these emanations, thinking of them as subordinate gods. For Christian Gnostics, Christ himself was an emanation from the divine Being over him. Here was the secret *gnosis,* knowledge, which Christianity imparted and which brought salvation: Christ had come onto the world stage to lift man off of it and up to a higher level of existence.

(b) One form of Christian Gnosticism was *Docetism* (from Greek *dokéo,* 'seem'). This held that Christ, who is divine, could not really become a human being but only *seemed* to do so. He seemed to be fatigued or thirsty or in pain. On the cross he did not say, 'My God, my God' but 'My power, my power, why hast thou forsaken me?' Notice, here, how the earliest Christian heretics did not deny that Jesus was divine. They denied that he was human.

(c) Coming closer to our own day, even standard Protestantism seems, now and again, to play down the material side of life, or to depreciate human effort. John Calvin, a leader of the Reformation who lived from 1509 to 1564, taught that human life is 'totally depraved.' That is, we have no ability to believe or to repent on our own. God alone can take any steps on our behalf.

In churches with a Calvinist background, worship is often less colorful than elsewhere. Holy Communion is likely to occur less frequently. Some sects hold that baptism is not really necessary. Do these features imply a tendency to look down on matter, or suggest that created things are, in themselves, unfit for use by their Creator?

(d) Calvinism is reflected in a recent movement called 'neo-orthodoxy' or 'neo-supernaturalism.' This declares that God is *wholly other* than the world of time and things. The world of time and things is totally depraved, and nothing in it is capable of turning toward Him. Instead, He breaks in upon us, from outside. He annihilates man's sinful world, and affronts and utterly overthrows man's intellect. That is bound to be the case, we are told, because the human mind is just as amiss as everything else, and cannot think straight. Notice how different this assertion is from one that we have previously made.[2] We have said that man's understanding is limited, that he cannot perceive all the truth in a single view, and therefore gets tangled up in absurd and fearful situations. Neo-orthodoxy does not stop there. It says that our intellects are not merely limited, but perversely antagonistic to God—so perverse that we *must always* come up with the wrong answer.[3] Our minds have no power at all to turn to God, and to us His truth, which is the real truth, must always seem false. But is this not a self-refuting proposition? Can we use reasoning to prove that all reasoning is false? If man's mind *always* gets a wrong answer, then neo-orthodoxy must be wrong too!

(e) Neo-orthodoxy is a gloomy religion, born in a

[2] Above, pages 13f.; 145ff.

[3] This idea had a bizarre result some years ago. The annual Gifford Lectures at the University of Edinburgh are on *natural theology,* that is, they are supposed to show how religious truths can be deduced from the study of nature. (Example: Since the universe exhibits plan or design, there must be a Great Designer.) But Karl Barth, a leading neo-orthodox theologian, used his Gifford Lectures to argue that nature and man's mind are depraved and can tell us nothing about God—i.e., natural theology is impossible!

gloomy time. It may seem strange, therefore, to compare it with such cheerful faiths as Christian Science, New Thought, Unity, or the so-called 'Science of Mind.' Yet these also say that the present world, of material things and events, is impermanent, ungodly and without validity; that God's only effect upon it is to bring it to nothingness; and that human action by itself is meaningless and futile. Like the Gnostics of old, these cults add that man is saved by their special, divinely imparted *knowledge*.[4]

All the foregoing movements, though they differ widely from one another, are prone to despise physical things and physical happenings. They all try to find *in Christianity* the ground for their despising. Most of us have encountered sects, or individuals, that do this. Perhaps there are practices, even within one's own Church, that might lead the unwary to look down on material things and to disvalue outward circumstances. Indeed nearly everybody is tempted to feel, now and then, that spiritual affairs are somehow *better* or *more true* than physical ones.

The New Testament says no such thing.

[4] Theosophy, too, says things like this; but it stems from Buddhism, not Christianity.

CHAPTER XIX

THINGS ARE SACRED

The New Testament does not place its faith exclusively in spirit, nor exclusively in matter. Instead, it makes the startling assertion that *matter and spirit are inseparable,* and that *both are sacred.*

Behind that assertion lay a way of looking at the world. It was different from the Greek way, and different in large measure from our modern way. The Greek had been used to thinking in abstract terms. So are we, and we use many words ending in *-ness* (goodness, happiness), *-ty* (beauty, liberty, purity), *-th* (truth, health) and the like. It is hard to say whether a people's way of thinking depends on the language they use, or whether they develop their language to fit their mental disposition: perhaps the latter. In either case, there is a close connection between a nation's language and the way its people look at life.

The Hebrew language was poor in abstract nouns. The Hebrew-Jewish mind thought far more regularly in down-to-earth, concrete and pictorial ways. For example, the Old Testament says not a word about the 'omnipotence' or 'transcendence' of God, but a great deal about 'his mighty hand and outstretched arm.' It has no abstract discussions of 'Divine Love.' It says, 'Like as a father pitieth his children, so the Lord pitieth them that revere him,' and 'As one whom his mother comforteth, so will I comfort you, saith the Lord.'[1] This pictorial way of thinking and writing is typical of the whole Bible. What is more, it is psychologically sound. All of us think more readily about concrete objects than about intangible generalities. The most sophisticated adult probably finds 'Santa Claus' an easier concept than 'the spirit of Christmas.' It is true to say, 'God is omnipresent Love.' It is just as true, but more rousing, more compelling, to look at Christ on his cross and say, 'God is like that.'

Yet it was not merely that the Jew used pictures where the Greek used long words. The Jew was convinced, further, that *God really does things.* God works in His world, and He works at it. The universe is a creation; that is, God made it. He is still here. He is still very much alive. He takes His material creation very seriously.

The early Christian believed so too; but he carried his conviction farther than had the Jew. This, indeed, is the crowning assertion of New Testament religion. God, in Christ, comes to transfigure the world and make it His own. Whether He will rejuvenate the present heaven and earth, or replace them with new ones,[2] in either case there will be a physical order, sacred to Him. Therefore, to writers of the New Testament, matter and history must not be despised. Nor may they be worshipped. They are to be redeemed.

Thus, caught up between matter and spirit, the early Christian seized both horns of the dilemma: he saw that both are true. Today it is still the Christian aim to imbue matter, and history, and everything around us, with the everliving Spirit of God. For there can be no uncertainty whatever that the physical world and the world of the

[1] Psalm 103:13; Isaiah 66:13.
[2] Compare above, pages 76ff.

spirit both are valid. 'I believe in one God,' say Roman Catholics and Eastern Orthodox and members of reformed Churches the world around, 'the Father Almighty, Maker of *heaven and earth*, And of *all things visible and invisible*.' God stands at the threshold of our physical and social life, poised to enter it, fill it with Himself and make it holy. Archbishop Temple once called Christianity 'the most avowedly materialist of all the great religions.'[3] It is. It is also the most spiritual religion in the world.

So the polarity of New Testament faith once more comes sharply home. Everywhere you touch it, in almost every typical phrase, it declares that matter and spirit must come together. That conviction is implicit in nearly all that we have said up to this point:

1. Christianity is the religion of the New Covenant, the new Israel, the Body of Christ. That is, *Christianity is an ecclesiastical religion.*

It is unfortunate that the words 'ecclesiastical' and 'ecclesiasticism' have, for some people, acquired a bad sense. These terms do not mean dry formality, or unsavory church politics, or backward and grasping priests imposing their wills on society! To call Christianity ecclesiastical is, in fact, to say something about God. In order to reach and redeem humanity, God sets within its midst this chosen community, or people, or Church, to be His instrument. It is His means by which history, the ongoing life of mankind, is to be endowed with His will and Spirit. To be a Christian is to be ecclesiastical, for it is to live and pray not *I* but *we*. There is no other Christianity than that. And that means in turn that the world of human happenings is meaningful to God.

2. *Christianity is an eschatological religion.* This again

[3] William Temple, *Nature, Man and God* (London, Macmillan, 1935), page 478.

says something about God: His purpose is not to be gain-
said. His will must and shall be done. Note, however, that
His purpose is a purpose for this world. So eschatology,
like ecclesiasticism, says that this world, these things,
this history, are of concern to the Eternal. Furthermore,
history is moving toward a divinely set consummation.
Just now, much of man's life is out of touch with divine
things, or at best the contacts seem sporadic and frag-
mentary. That shall not for ever be the case. The life of
mankind must come into contact, yes into full association
and union, with God.

There is another facet to eschatology, which some New
Testament writers touched on. The eternal purpose embraces not only all humanity, but the whole universe.
How this could be, or what God's plan for the physical
world is, they do not clearly say; but the conviction
itself they assert roundly:[4]

And I saw a new heaven and a new earth: for the first heaven
and the first earth are passed away. And he that sitteth upon
the throne said, Behold, I make *all things* new.

The heavens that now are, and the earth, by the same word
have been stored up for fire, being reserved against the day
of judgment. But forget not this one thing, beloved, that one
day is with the Lord as a thousand years, and a thousand
years as one day. But the day of the Lord will come; in the
which the heavens shall pass away with a great noise, the
elements shall be dissolved with fervent heat, and the earth
and the works that are therein. But according to his promise,
we look for new heavens and a new earth, wherein dwelleth
righteousness.

In those days, after that tribulation, the sun shall be
darkened, and the moon shall not give her light, and the
stars shall be falling from heaven, and the powers that are

[4] The following quotations are from Revelation 21:1,5; II Peter 3:7-13;
Mark 13:24-26.

in the heavens shall be shaken. And then shall they see the son of man coming in clouds with great power and glory.

In part, such language is another pictorial way of describing God's awe-inspiring majesty and plan. Yet behind these passages lies a conviction. When man, the noblest figure in creation, goes wrong, he involves all creation with him. His sin is sin against the Infinite God and it sets the universe awry. Therefore the 'wrath' of God—a goodness and purity so perfect that nothing wrong can remain in His presence—must embrace the whole universe. All creation, says St. Paul, must await the final accomplishment of His design:

The creation waits with eager longing for the revealing of the sons of God; for the creation was subjected to futility, not of its own will but by the will of him who subjected it . . . ; the creation itself will be set free from its bondage to decay and obtain the glorious liberty of the children of God. We know that the whole creation has been groaning in travail together until now; and not only the creation, but we ourselves, who have the first fruits of the Spirit, groan inwardly as we wait for adoption as sons, the redemption of our bodies. (*Romans 8:19-23, RSV*)

3. *Christianity is a social gospel.* It began among the common people. Ever since, when the common people have been degraded, and when Christianity has been true to itself, it has gone out to them.

Objectors have not been lacking, who raised serious questions about this side of Christianity. For one thing, Jesus said little or nothing against the monstrous social ills of his time—war, slavery, child labor, unfair taxation, the low position of women—and he offered no panaceas for them. Should we preach a social gospel, it is asked, if he did not? For another thing, in discussing economics and politics Christian leaders can, unless they are specially trained, get into areas where others know more than they do. Or they may seem to identify Christianity with a particular, and usually passing, economic theory. Some have even been accused, rightly or wrongly, of preaching social reform only because there was little else in Christianity that they really believed!

None of these objections touch the heart of the matter. Like ecclesiasticism and eschatology, Christian social concern stems from the basic recognition: *The world around us must be neither ignored, nor escaped from, nor succumbed to. It must be redeemed.* Perhaps Jesus did not discuss isolated social evils or their cure.[5] Yet from first to last his thoughts and his life were with the socially needy: publicans and harlots at John's Baptism, publicans and sinners at table in Galilee, common people by the lake, the sick in body and mind, thieves on crosses next to his own. Even his eschatology, like the Jewish eschatology before him, showed his anxiety about the poor and the distressed.[6]

The fact of history is that everywhere Christianity has gone it has opened people's eyes to envisage a new world, has brought moral concern for human need, and has inspired social upheaval. When society goes wrong, or there is war, or civilization goes to pot, we say that Christianity has failed. We do not say that Buddhism or Hinduism or Taoism or Islam has failed. There is a profound reason. Alone among the religions of the earth, Christianity feels a world-wide mission and bears a responsibility for all of society, and all of history. For there cannot be any part of man's life, anywhere, ever, that is exempt from the Christ.

4. *Christianity is a sacramental religion.* There are

[5] Though see his teaching against divorce, Matthew 5:31-32; 19:3-12.
[6] Compare above, pages 74ff.

many definitions of 'sacrament.' Some think of it as a
religious ceremony with strong overtones, it may be, of
sentiment and of association with the past. To others a
sacrament is a memorial, a kind of souvenir to remind
them of Christ the Lord. Or is it a symbol or mark, of
something that has happened to us inwardly, perhaps
like the diploma which shows that I am 'educated' or the
ring indicating that I am married? Or does 'sacrament'
mean that we take something we own, like bread or wine
or water, offer it to God and, in spirit, offer ourselves to
Him too?

All these statements are true. They are not, however,
the whole truth or even the most important part of it.
For 'sacrament' means that *God takes the physical thing*,
invests *that* with Himself, and makes *that* a vehicle
whereby He comes to us. In a sacrament we do offer
ourselves to Him; but He likewise offers Himself to us.
Thus 'sacrament' says more than 'ecclesiastical' or 'eschatology' or 'social gospel' can say. In those, God's coming could be a hope for the future, or an activity still
incomplete. In sacrament, God comes *now*. In those
others, the material world awaits expectantly to be seized
by the divine. In a sacrament God takes this thing that
I see with my eyes now, touch with my fingers now, and
makes it His own.

Of course, God comes to us spiritually, too—in the
quiet of our consciences, in our prayers, in a hundred
other ways. Sacrament does not deny spiritual religion.
It adds to it a new truth. If the everlasting God meets
me in a flash of my mind, He can meet me also in the
thing in my hand. And why should He not? Did He not
make them both, and does He not cherish them both?

The sacrament may be the Holy Communion, of the
bread and wine 'of the new Covenant.' That is why

people sometimes speak of 'the real Presence' of God or Christ there. It may be the water that pours over one at Baptism. Or it *might* be any other thing. For the eternal God can take *any thing* He has created, and make that thing His Holy of Holies.

CHAPTER XX

THE WHOLE MAN

When the New Testament says that matter and spirit must come together, it is not talking just in broad generalizations. It is saying something very definite about you and me. To every man, woman and child, the most immediate physical fact is his own body, and the most immediate spiritual fact is his own mind or soul. These, says the New Testament, belong together. Your body and your soul are alike sacred to God. To our western, European minds this idea has some startling implications.

First of all, consider what the New Testament, and particularly St. Paul, has to say about human physique. Here, once more, the faith is expressed in polarities, because there is no other way to put it. When, for example, St. Paul uses the word 'flesh,' he at times appears to look down on it. In fact if some of his sentences are taken out of their contexts, he sounds almost like a Gnostic or a Hindu:[1]

The infirmity of your flesh.

I know that in me, that is, in my flesh, dwelleth no good thing.

They that are in the flesh cannot please God. . . . Brethren, we are debtors, not to the flesh, to live after the flesh: for

[1] Romans 6:19; 7:18; 8:8-13; 13:14; I Corinthians 1:26-31; 15:50; II Corinthians 10:3-4; Galatians 5:16-24; Philippians 3:3.

if ye live after the flesh, ye must die; but if by the Spirit, ye shall live.

Make not provision for the flesh, to fulfill the lusts thereof.

Not many wise after the flesh [are called to be Christian] . . . that no flesh should glory before God. . . .

Flesh and blood cannot inherit the kingdom of God.

We do not war according to the flesh. For the weapons of our warfare are not of the flesh, but mighty before God to the casting down of strongholds.

I say, Walk by the Spirit, and ye shall not fulfil the lust of the flesh. For the flesh lusteth against the Spirit, and the Spirit against the flesh; for these are contrary the one to the other . . . And they that are of Christ Jesus have crucified the flesh with the passions and the lusts thereof.

We worship by the Spirit of God, and . . . have no confidence in the flesh.

Nor was Paul the only one to express himself in this way.[2]

And Jesus answered, Blessed art thou, Simon Bar-Jonah: for flesh and blood hath not revealed it unto thee [that I am the Messiah], but my Father who is in heaven.

The spirit indeed is willing, but the flesh is weak.

As many as received him, to them gave he the right to become children of God, even to them that were born not of the will of the flesh, but of God.

Except one be born of the Spirit, he cannot enter into the kingdom of God. That which is born of the flesh is flesh; and that which is born of the Spirit is spirit.

Jesus said unto them, It is the spirit that giveth life; the flesh profiteth nothing: the words that I have spoken unto you are spirit, and are life.

[2] See Matthew 16:17; Mark 14:38; John 1:12-13; 3:5-6; 6:63; I Peter 3:18; 4:2. Several of these are abridged here.

Christ also suffered, that he might bring us to God; being put to death in the flesh, but made alive in the spirit.

Ye no longer should live the rest of your time in the flesh to the lusts of men, but to the will of God.

However, when we read these passages in their contexts we discover that they do not condemn skin and bones—physical objects—for their own sakes. What is condemned is the wrong attitude toward physique. St. Paul, especially, was revolted by the license and sensuous indulgence that were all around him in the Mediterranean world. Like the others he said that exclusive devotion to things material is hurtful and wrong. It is hurtful and wrong because our physical nature is a sacred possession which God has given us. To use it in an ungodly way is to do violence to ourselves. We cannot do that with impunity.

Yet a deeper thought is implied here. What is true of every other created thing is true of man's physique too. It is potentially a Holy of holies, a 'temple of the Holy Spirit' as St. Paul put it (*I Corinthians 6:19*). Flesh and spirit, like matter and spirit everywhere, must come together. It is when the bodily and the spiritual are kept apart, when the Spirit is denied access and physique tries to go its own way, that 'flesh' becomes an evil thing. This stupid ignoring of the divine in our physical concerns, this monstrous hope to keep God out—the worse for being often an unconscious hope—St. Paul calls the 'mind of the flesh':

They that are after the flesh mind the things of the flesh; but they that are after the Spirit the things of the Spirit. For the mind of the flesh is death; but the mind of the Spirit is life and peace: because the mind of the flesh is enmity against God; for it is not subject to the law of God, neither indeed can be. (*Romans 8:5-9; 12:2*)

'Therefore,' he says,

Be not fashioned according to this world: but be ye transformed by the renewing of your mind, that ye may prove what is the good and well-pleasing and perfect will of God.

A similar thought is expressed in Ephesians:[3]

No longer walk as the Gentiles also walk, in the vanity of their mind, being darkened in their understanding, alienated from the life of God, because of the ignorance that is in them . . . who gave themselves up to work all uncleanness with greediness. But ye did not so learn Christ; if so be that ye heard him, and were taught in him, even as the truth is in Jesus: that ye put away, as concerning your former manner of life, the old man, that waxeth corrupt . . . and that ye be renewed in the spirit of your mind, and put on the new man, that is after God, created in righteousness and holiness of truth.

The 'mind of the flesh' is devilish. Yet our physical nature is by no means *inherently* opposed to God. On the contrary, flesh can be endowed with Spirit, yes, even to the point of God Himself coming 'in the flesh':[4]

In the beginning was the Word, and the Word was with God, and the Word was God. . . . And the Word became flesh, and dwelt among us, and we beheld his glory.

. . . that the life also of Jesus may be manifested in our body . . . that the life also of Jesus may be manifested in our mortal flesh.

And without controversy great is the mystery of godliness:
He who was manifested in the flesh,
Justified in the spirit,
Seen of angels,

[3] See Ephesians 4:17-24. Ephesians differs from Paul's other letters, and some scholars think it was written not by him, but in his name by one of his devoted followers. Such a procedure would have been quite acceptable in the first century; compare above, pages 73ff.
[4] John 1:1,14; II Corinthians 4:10-12; I Timothy 3:16; I John 4:2-3. Compare John 6:48-58.

Preached among the nations,
Believed on in the world,
Received up into glory.

Every spirit that confesseth that Jesus Christ is come in
the flesh is of God: and every spirit that confesseth not Jesus
is not of God.

The last was in direct answer to the Gnostics and Doce-
tists, who held that physique is evil in itself, and that
Christ could not come in full physical humanity but only
seemed to do so.

St. Paul seldom used 'flesh' in this good sense, as being
potentially the dwelling place of God. Perhaps this was
because he had to discuss the bad sense so frequently.
When he thought of man's physical nature made holy by
the Spirit, or waiting to be made holy, he usually preferred the word 'body': [5]

I beseech you therefore, brethren, by the mercies of God, to
present your bodies a living sacrifice, holy, acceptable to God,
which is your spiritual service.

The body is for the Lord; and the Lord for the body: and
God both raised the Lord, and will raise up us through his
power. Know ye not that your bodies are members of Christ?
Or know ye not that your body is a temple of the Holy Spirit
which is in you? Glorify God therefore in your body.

Christ shall be magnified in my body, whether by life, or
by death.

Our citizenship is in heaven; whence also we wait for a
Saviour, the Lord Jesus Christ: who shall fashion anew the
body of our humiliation, that it may be conformed to the body
of his glory, according to the working whereby he is able
even to subject all things unto himself.

[5] See Romans 12:1-2; I Corinthians 6:12-20; Philippians 1:19-26;
3:18-21. See also Romans 8:22-23. These and the next two groups of
quotations are abridged.

The body is for the Lord—and the Lord for the body! So high is the body's worth that it becomes a symbol for some of the loftiest concepts in the New Testament. In picturing the New Israel under the New Covenant, the figure that thrilled St. Paul most, and was heaviest with indescribable meaning, was that of the Body of Christ. As a foot or hand cannot live by itself, no more can the Christian live to himself. More, the community of Christians is, in a most real way, an extension of Christ's own life in the world, breathing his spirit and doing his work.[6]

For even as we have many members in one body, and all the members have not the same office: so we, who are many, are one body in Christ, and severally members one of another.

For as the body is one, and hath many members, and all the members of the body, being many, are one body; so also is Christ. For in one Spirit were we all baptized into one body, whether Jews or Greeks, whether bond or free; and were all made to drink of one Spirit. Now ye are the body of Christ, and severally members thereof.

And he [Christ] is the head of the body, the church . . . the Head, from whom all the body, being supplied and knit together through the joints and bands, increaseth with the increase of God . . . Let the peace of Christ rule in your hearts, to the which also ye were called in one body; and be ye thankful.

The church is his body, the fulness of him that filleth all in all.

Most hallowed of all, 'body' brought back the figure of Christ himself.[7]

Jesus said to them, Destroy this temple, and in three days I will raise it up. The Jews said, Forty and six years was this

[6] See Romans 12:4-5; I Corinthians 12:4-27; Colossians 1:18; 2:19; 3:15; also Ephesians 1:22-23. Compare above, pages 49ff.
[7] John 2:19-21; I Corinthians 11:23-29; 10:15ff. See also the stories of the Last Supper, Matthew 26:17-29; Mark 14:12-25; Luke 22:7-30.

temple in building, and wilt thou raise it up in three days? But he spake of the temple of his body.

The Lord Jesus, in the night in which he was betrayed, took bread; and when he had given thanks, he brake it, and said, This is my body, which is broken for you: this do in remembrance of me . . . For as often as ye eat this bread . . . ye proclaim the Lord's death till he come. Wherefore whosoever shall eat the bread . . . in an unworthy manner, shall be guilty of the body . . . of the Lord. But let a man prove himself, and so let him eat of the bread.

The bread which we break, is it not a communion of the body of Christ? seeing that we, who are many, are one bread, one body: for we are all partakers of the one bread.

What is man? Nowhere can the New Testament offend the western mind more, than in its answer to that question. Is man an invisible, permanent soul encased in a visible but temporary physical garment? Is the body less important, less good than the soul? Western man has often answered, Yes. The New Testament answers, No! You cannot thus cut man in two. His physique is as significant and sacred as his mind and, if man is to live, these may not be parted.

This brings us to the early Christians' views about life after death. Their teaching may trouble us. Today there are Christians, born and brought up in the Church, who do not realize what the New Testament says on this subject. Some people, when they find it out, are shocked and dismayed. For the New Testament says almost nothing about the immortality of the soul. Instead, it talks about the resurrection of the body.[8]

As so often elsewhere, New Testament belief in life be-

---

[8] Greek *anastasis*, 'resurrection,' occurs 38 times in the New Testament. *Aphtharsia* and *athanasia*, both translated 'immortality,' occur just twice and 3 times respectively. The expression 'immortality of the soul' does not appear at all.

yond death was rooted solidly in the Old Testament. Again like other Christian convictions, it had lowly origins. For a long, long time the Hebrew people had supposed that this life is all there is for man:[9]

Verily every man at his best state is altogether vanity. . . .
O spare me, that I may recover strength,
Before I go hence, and be no more.

The dead praise not the Lord,
Neither any that go down into silence.

The living know that they shall die: but the dead know not anything, neither have they any more a reward; for the memory of them is lost. Also their love, and their hatred, and their envy, is now perished; neither have they any more a portion for ever in any thing.

In fact, according to the Garden of Eden story, God deliberately barred man from immortality. Adam and Eve were expelled *not* because they had disobeyed, but to keep them from getting another fruit that would give them life for ever:[10]

And the Lord God said, Behold, the man is become as one of us, to know good and evil: and now, lest he put forth his hand and take also of the tree of life, and eat, and live for ever . . . So he drove out the man, and he placed at the east of the garden of Eden the cherubim, and the flame of a sword which turned every way, to keep the way of the tree of life.

Lacking faith in a future existence, the Hebrew supposed, of course, that rewards and punishments are limited to this world. For living uprightly, a man might be awarded a good old age, or wealth, or many descendants:[11]

[9] Psalms 39:5,13; 115:17; Ecclesiastes 9:5-6. Compare Ecclesiastes 3:19-20; 8:8.
[10] Genesis 3:22-24, ERV.
[11] Genesis 22:16-18; Exodus 20:12; Deuteronomy 8:1; Psalm 91:14-16.

By myself have I sworn, saith the Lord, because thou hast done this [act of devoted obedience to the Lord], I will multiply thy descendants as the stars of the heaven, and as the sand upon the seashore.

Honor thy father and thy mother: that thy days may be long on the land which the Lord thy God giveth thee.

All the commandments which I command thee this day shall ye observe to do, that ye may live, and multiply, and go in and possess the land which the Lord sware unto your fathers.

Because he hath set his love upon me. . . .
With long life will I satisfy him.

Even the line of the beloved 23rd Psalm, 'I shall dwell in the house of the Lord *for ever*,' originally meant 'down to old age.'

Then, perhaps from contact with Egypt, Israelites got the notion of a place under the ground, where the spirits of the departed went. It was called *Sheol*, which is rendered 'Hades' in some English Bibles, 'the grave' in others. This was what King David had in mind when he said of his deceased son, 'I shall go to him but he shall not return to me.' [12] At best, Sheol offered only a dreary half-existence, with none of the hope that 'immortality' or 'resurrection' conveyed to later generations. To the Hebrew mind a 'disembodied spirit' was sickly and futile, and could not partake of the full nature of a man. (Does the word 'ghost' evoke something of the same feeling today?) This attitude is reflected in the New Testament too. After his resurrection, our Lord tells his friends that *he is more than a spirit; that he is himself*:[13]

They were terrified and affrighted, and supposed that they had beheld a spirit. And he said unto them, Why are ye

[12] This was the son of David and Bath-Sheba. See II Samuel 12:15-23.
[13] See Luke 24:36-44.

troubled? See my hands and my feet, that it is *I myself:* handle me, and see; for a spirit hath not flesh and bones as ye behold *me* having. And when he had said this, he showed them his hands and his feet

and, as further demonstration, he ate before them.

With long centuries of defeat and grief came Israel's growing conviction that God, who is just, would redress His people's wrongs. But then, what of Israel's martyrs, and all the rest who had died without justice being done them? What, also, of Israel's enemies, who enjoyed their ill-gotten gains and had not been punished for their misdeeds? A virtuous God could not let all that inequity stand. So they came to believe that, at the Day of the Lord, God would *resurrect* those who had died. He would mete out full justice, scourging the wicked with the rod of His anger, but enabling His faithful ones to share in the Kingdom:[14]

And many of them that sleep in the dust of the earth shall awake, some to everlasting life, and some to shame and everlasting contempt.

Thus the doctrine of the resurrection came, like so much else, out of Covenant thinking and out of eschatology. Belief in the resurrection was not universal among Jews of Jesus' day. Some accepted, instead, the Greek idea of immortality of the soul.[15] Others continued to believe that this life is all there is. Even when a resurrection was believed in, the conviction never reached the heights in Judaism that it achieved in the New Testament. Yet the ground of the new faith is plain to be seen in the old. For both Testaments are certain that God reigns; that He is just, and will not leave His children to

[14] See Daniel 12:1-4.
[15] See, for example, the Wisdom of Solomon, an Old Testament apocryphal book written about 150 B.C.

be defeated by death; and that a man must have and keep a physical nature to be a man at all.

At this point perhaps you are growing skeptical. It is all very well to show where the New Testament concept came from. What, however, does it mean in the concrete situation? Are the molecules of my body to be pieced together again, some years or some centuries hence? And *which* molecules, seeing that my bodily substance changes every few years—those when I was eight, or eighteen, or eighty? Furthermore, if 'disembodied ghost' is a distasteful notion, what about 'resurrected corpse'?

If we ask the New Testament lugubrious questions like these, we shall get no answer. Here again, the western mind pokes and prods, and asks, '*How* does God work it?' where the New Testament mind asked, more sanely, '*What* has God wrought?' The answer to *that* question echoes again and again:[16]

Verily, verily, I say unto you . . . As the Father hath life in himself, even so gave he to the Son also to have life in himself: and he gave him authority to execute judgment, because he is a son of man. Marvel not at this: for the hour cometh, in which all that are in the tombs shall hear his voice, and shall come forth; they that have done good, unto the resurrection of life; and they that have done evil, unto the resurrection of judgment.

Jesus said, I am the resurrection and the life: he that believeth on me, though he die, yet shall he live: and whosoever liveth and believeth on me shall never die.

Now hath Christ been raised from the dead, and become the first fruits of them that are asleep. For since by man came death, by man came also the resurrection of the dead.

[16] John 5:25-29; 11:25; I Corinthians 15:20-23 (but read the whole chapter); II Timothy 1:10; 2:8,11-12. Compare Mark 12:18-27.

For as in Adam all die, even so in Christ shall all be made alive. But each in his own order: Christ the first fruits; then they that are Christ's, at his coming.

Our Saviour Jesus Christ, who abolished death, and brought life and immortality to light through the gospel.

Remember Jesus Christ, risen from the dead . . . If we died with him, we shall also live with him: if we endure, we shall also reign with him.

A resurrection awaits us. As to the *how* of it, some writers did use pictorial language which we can read, for example, in *Revelation* or *I Corinthians* or *I Thessalonians*. Always, however, they knew that that future is utterly beyond our power to imagine:

But some one will say, How are the dead raised? and with what manner of body do they come? Thou foolish one! That which thou sowest is not quickened, except it die: and that which thou sowest, thou sowest not the body that shall be, but a bare grain . . . But God giveth it a body as it pleased him . . . Behold, I tell you a mystery.

We speak God's wisdom in a mystery, the wisdom that hath been hidden, which God foreordained before the worlds unto our glory; which none of the princes of this world hath known: for had they known it, they would not have crucified the Lord of glory: but as it is written,
Things which eye saw not, and ear heard not,
And which entered not into the heart of man,
Whatsoever things God prepared for them that love him.
(I Corinthians 15:35ff;2:7-9)

There is a remarkable parallel between the mystery of the future life and the mystery of the future of Israel. The old Israel dies now, but it too must rise again, to hail the Messiah whom it has refused. Here once more one gets the strong impression that the fate of the individual believer cannot be separated from the fate of God's beloved community. They must be saved together:[17]

They asked him, saying, Lord, dost thou at this time restore the kingdom to Israel? And he said unto them, It is not for you to know the times or the seasons, which the Father hath set within his own authority.

I would not, brethren, have you ignorant of this mystery, lest ye be wise in your own conceits, that a hardening in part hath befallen Israel, until the fulness of the Gentiles be come in; and so all Israel shall be saved. . . .

O the depth of the riches both of the wisdom and the knowledge of God! how unsearchable are his judgments, and his ways past tracing out!

The future life is a mystery. Yet four clear convictions do emerge from the New Testament books. (1) The end of this life means the dissolution of soul from body. Whether the spirit then remains 'awake' or 'asleep'—and they were not sure about that—it is 'unclothed,' as St. Paul says, and incomplete. Thus death, the disjoining of what ought to be joined, is really death. It comes to all men, and 'only God hath immortality' (*I Timothy 6:16*). Death is our enemy, the worst enemy of all.

(2) The life beyond will involve the whole person, and not just his separated spirit. This means that, whatever the process by which it comes about, there will be something corresponding to physique. We shall be 'not unclothed, but clothed upon.' 'God giveth it a body as it pleaseth him.' Changed it will be, and invigorated, splendid, incorrupt beyond our wildest dreams. But it will be a body. That is why the Christian, knowing that he speaks far past his power to picture, still says, 'I believe in the resurrection of the body and the life everlasting.'

[17] Acts 1:6-7; Romans 11:25-36. On the mystery of the chosen people, compare the discussion of Mark 4:26-29, page 163 above.

For God created physique. He cannot despise what He has made, but must and will endow it with His eternal Spirit.

(3) *Death is conquered now.* As a mere occurrence it keeps happening, of course, to us as to all living creatures. But the *sting*, the fright of it is gone. The Christian *knows* that his life is hid with Christ in God. This Christian confidence is no mere theory. It is the soberest fact, which every clergyman meets constantly. People steeped in Christianity usually face death, their own or their loved ones', with a serenity and a stability that are sorrowfully lacking elsewhere.

(4) *Now* are we the sons of God. In a most important sense we are incorrupt *now*. So, these early Christians urged, live incorruptly *now*.

Here is the ground for Christian moral behavior, on which the New Testament stands. Our bodies, as dear to God as our spirits, must be kept ready for Him. Further, in being baptized into this faith we have truly and in ourselves 'died with him, and risen with him.' Therefore we cannot but glorify God in our bodies, which are His.[18]

If then ye were raised together with Christ, seek the things that are above . . . For ye died, and your life is hid with Christ in God. When Christ, who is our life, shall be manifested, then shall ye also with him be manifested in glory. . . . And whatsoever ye do, in word or in deed, do all in the name of the Lord Jesus, giving thanks to God the Father through him.

He hath granted unto us his precious and exceeding great promises; that through these ye may become partakers of the divine nature, having escaped from the corruption that is in the world.

Behold what manner of love the Father hath bestowed upon us, that we should be called children of God; and such we

[18] Colossians 3:1-17; II Peter 1:4; I John 3:1-3. Compare Romans 6:4-6.

are. For this cause the world knoweth us not, because it knew him not. Beloved, now are we children of God, and it is not yet made manifest what we shall be. We know that, if he shall be manifested, we shall be like him; for we shall see him even as he is. And every one that hath this hope set on him purifieth himself, even as he is pure.

'We know.' That phrase or one like it has sounded over and over again in the passages we have studied: 'I know,' 'ye may prove,' 'ye have been taught by him, as the truth is,' 'without controversy,' 'behold and see.' Why were they so confident? What had convinced them? May we, too, know? The tales of Mount Olympus are all but forgotten: is Christianity more than just another myth, to be forgotten in its turn? The arguments of a Plato might convince the intellect but they could not transfigure a world: then is Christian picture language not just easier to follow, but more trustworthy than the best logic of man's mind? Where, O God, is the proof? Where is *Thy* warrant that these things be true?

THE SIXTH KEY:

THE MAN

CHAPTER XXI

THE VICTOR

Like all men everywhere, Jesus' disciples had sought to interpret the new and strange by the old they already knew. Naturally, they wondered whether he might be the Messiah—for everybody, especially in Galilee, was talking about Messiah, and nearly every one hoped he would come soon.

Then when they were sure he was indeed the One, they were bound to try to see in him what folklore and patriotism had taught them to look for. Their prejudgments had bred a kind of spiritual myopia, and they could not see the vista toward which Jesus so urgently pointed. They had called him Messiah, Christ. He had welcomed it. At once they thought (as who of us would not?) of their own privileged position as princes in the new Kingdom. They vied for the top places, until Jesus had to tell them, 'He who is greatest among you must be your servant.'[1]

Then Jesus was arrested, and to their self-seeking the disciples added craven fear. In fright for their own lives, they cringed like hunted beasts in whatever hole they could find.

Then suddenly they were cowards no longer. They

[1] Mark 10:43-44. Similar admonitions are recorded on numerous occasions: see Mark 9:33-35; Matthew 23:8-12; Luke 22:24-27.

stood and hurled at Jesus' judges the challenge that he
had risen from death itself, and that he would live for
evermore.[2]

Him God raised up the third day, and gave him to be made
manifest . . . unto witnesses that were chosen before of God,
even to us, who ate and drank with him after he rose from
the dead.

Blessed be the God and Father of our Lord Jesus Christ,
who according to his great mercy begat us again unto a
living hope by the resurrection of Jesus Christ from the dead.

If Christ hath not been raised, then . . . we are of all men
most pitiable. But now hath Christ been raised from the dead,
the firstfruits of them that are asleep.

Him God hath raised from the dead . . . Therefore repent.

They claimed to have Jesus' own words, spoken both before and after he rose from death:[3]

No sign shall be given unto this generation but the sign of
Jonah the prophet. For as Jonah was three days in the belly of
the sea-monster, so shall the son of man be three days in the
heart of the earth.

I am the Living one; and I was dead, and behold I am alive
for evermore.

Many authors in discussing the Resurrection have
pointed out the change it made in the spirit of the disciples. It is right to point that out. It is one proof that their
experience of their risen Lord was true. There is, however,
another way to look at it. In the black days following
Gethsemane these men were not just afraid; they were
bitterly disillusioned. All the world could see how wrong
they had been, how unfit Jesus was for their trust. May
not some of them have thought, Judas was right? Thus

[2] Acts 10:40-41; I Peter 1:3; I Corinthians 15:14-20; Acts 3:15, 19.
[3] Matthew 12:39-40; Revelation 1:18.

the Resurrection destroyed not only their selfish cowardice, but their crude theology. No longer would they try to mold Jesus to their pattern. Now he molded them. A scarce two months after Jesus' death we find the disciples, now turned Apostles, preaching everywhere that Jesus is Lord. He is at the right hand of the Father. He is Judge of the world. From him, the ever-living and ever-present Messiah or Christ, flows the power of God down to the innermost recesses of man's being. Thus it was no mere change of mood or strengthening of fibre in these men. The spiritual distance they traveled, from that black Friday until the day St. Peter preached the first Christian sermon (*Acts 2:14-41*), was so vast that it marked, in fact, a new religion.

Here is why one modern effort to account for the Resurrection story must be rejected. It is sometimes supposed that the disciples believed in Jesus, they *knew* that his influence could never die, and this conviction gradually crystallized into tales that he had risen from death. That, however, is precisely what they did *not* know or believe. They had not grasped his meaning. They had been chagrined and humiliated on his account. It was the, not gradual, but sudden and staggering experience of events following his death which gave them the Christian faith.

So they preached that people should confess Jesus as Lord, and should repent and be baptized. Here we meet a strange circumstance. If a preacher nowadays desired his hearers to repent, he would very likely say, 'God is coming in judgment: therefore repent'; or, 'There is a hell for the sinner and a heaven for the good: therefore repent'; or, 'God has shown you what is right,' or, 'Christianity requires brotherly love: therefore repent.' The Apostles, however, did not stress those things. Understand it as we may, what they said was, 'God hath raised Jesus from the dead. *Therefore* repent.' They pointed out, of course, that Jesus' Resurrection proved him to be what they now said he was. Yet the Resurrection was no mere ground for *other* religious beliefs. *The Resurrection was, in itself, their message.*

It is a commonplace that when a dozen witnesses testify about an unusual occurrence, such as an accident, their stories will differ widely. Hence it need not surprise us that, with so astounding an event as Jesus' return from death, the accounts vary a good deal more than do those of his ministry. Still, the general outline is the same in all the Gospels.[4]

Most of the disciples had fled before Jesus was executed. A few women in his band (some of them, probably, wives of his male followers) had had more courage, and had gone out to the crucifixion ground. They stood at a distance, and saw what happened. It was, you will recall, the day before a very important Sabbath. The new day, Saturday or the Sabbath, would begin with the coming sunset. So as not to have bodies hanging on crosses over the sacred day, the soldiers made sure that all three condemned men die quickly. Late in the afternoon some acquaintances, who were not within Jesus' closest fellowship, took his body down from the cross and laid it in a near-by tomb. They did it hastily. With sunset approaching, there was not time for proper ministrations to the deceased.

On the Sabbath, work was of course forbidden. Early the next morning, Sunday, the women who had watched the crucifixion arose and went out to the tomb. They took along spices and ointments, to care properly for all

---

[4] Matthew 27:55-28:20; Mark 15:40-16:8; Luke 23:49-24:49; John 19:31-21:25; also Mark 16:9-20 which was added to the Gospel by a later hand.

that was left of their leader. When they reached the tomb, they found it empty. A figure whom they did not recognize was seated just inside the sepulchre entrance. He said to them, 'Why seek ye the living among the dead? He is not here. He is risen!' They rushed back to the city. Whether they told the disciples at once or whether they were at first afraid to tell, the Gospels are not agreed.

Soon, however, amazing things began to happen. Jesus appeared to Simon Peter. Toward evening he drew alongside two of the disciples as they were walking along the road. They did not know him, but they invited the stranger in for a meal. Then as he was breaking a piece of bread (perhaps something about his gesture caught their eye), they knew who he was. That evening he appeared to all eleven disciples; it may have been in the same upper room where they had had their last supper together. He told them to meet him again in Galilee.

They went soon to Galilee. There, on a hillside one day, they saw him and talked with him. 'All power,' he told them, 'is given unto me both in Heaven and on earth. Go ye and make disciples of all nations. And lo, I am with you always, even to the end of the world.'

For some forty days they kept meeting him like that (*Acts 1:2*). Some of his appearances were in Galilee, others in or near Jerusalem, until there almost seem to be two cycles of tradition about it all—one a 'Galilean' and one a 'Jerusalemite.' [5] For all the differences, there was no variance about the central fact. The Lord Jesus was alive, they had seen him, they had eaten and drunk with him. At this time, in these places, under these circumstances, these things had happened.

[5] Some scholars think this was indeed the case, and that the Galilean stories are more primitive than the Jerusalem ones.

Then after forty days they saw him no more.

What shall the modern mind say to all this? To continue to assert that a man really died and then really rose again—does that not offend against everything we have so painstakingly learned about our world? Is there not some way to explain or reinterpret the ancient tale, so as to make it fit better into modern patterns of thought? Can we keep, say, its great and noble lessons, without committing ourselves to it as an historical fact?

We can try. Remember that this was a credulous age, in which people saw miracles all around them. Before these men ever met Jesus, they had doubtless heard and believed many tales about rising from death. But precisely here is the difficulty: these other risings had not transformed people's character, nor sent men out to risk their lives and set the world by the ears. Jesus' Resurrection did. That is the plainest evidence that Jesus' Resurrection was *not* like the common run of superstition or fable.

The enemies of Christianity had, says the *Gospel of Matthew*, a simpler explanation. The disciples stole and hid Jesus' body, and then announced that he was alive again. Is this credible? What kind of minds must these people have had, that not just one or two of them but dozens should offer their lives to defend their own lie?

Well then, perhaps Jesus did not really die. After all, crucifixion damaged no vital organs. The victim might hang for many days before he succumbed to the hunger, thirst and cramping muscles. Yet Jesus was on the cross but a few hours. Let us say, then, that he merely swooned, and afterward in the cool quiet of the tomb revived. He escaped and returned to his erstwhile friends. This theory faces prodigious difficulties. It forgets the scourging. Victims often died under that, and one claiming to be 'King' would have been whipped mercilessly. It of course ignores the story in the Fourth Gospel, that to insure Jesus' death the soldiers thrust a spear into his side.[6] Worst of all, it takes the lie from the disciples and places it squarely upon Jesus himself. And if we find Jesus guilty of the deliberate and ghastly hoax, there is still a huge question: How could that beaten, wounded and ill figure have restored the confidence of his humiliated followers and roused their enthusiasm to fever pitch?

Or perhaps the women went to the wrong tomb. They were from Galilee, and probably did not know Jerusalem very well. Arriving at the wrong sepulchre, they were told that Jesus was not there—and their startled reaction set going the whole train of Christianity's mistaken faith. Yet they *had* watched Jesus' death and burial and, clearly, thought they knew where to go. Furthermore, could their hysteria, unbuttressed by other evidence, have been enough to reawaken the disciples' assurance? If we feel we can say 'Yes' to that, there is another, harder query. Very soon the Jerusalem authorities were doing everything they could think of to stamp Christianity out. The easiest way to nip this movement in the bud would have been simply to get the body of Jesus and display it. *Why didn't they?*

Many people have recognized how futile all these 'explanations' are, and have fallen back on another which seems, at first, a good deal more plausible. In the New Testament there are not four, but five accounts of the Resurrection. If we arrange these in the order in which they were written, it is evident that the later the story is (and therefore the further removed from what actually happened) the more miraculous it is:

[6] John 19:31-37. Some MSS. have a similar account at Matthew 27:49-50.

John (written *perhaps* about 100 A.D.): Mary Magdalene finds the tomb empty. She meets two angels.

Matthew (about 95 A.D.): Mary Magdalene and 'the other Mary' find the tomb empty, and meet one angel.

Luke (about 85 A.D.): The women find the tomb empty, and meet two men.

Mark (about 65 A.D.): The women find the tomb empty, and meet one man.

Paul (in *I Corinthians 15*, about 55 A.D.): No women are mentioned, and an empty tomb is not described.

Other features of the five accounts follow the same pattern. The closer we get to the actual date of the Resurrection, the fewer are the stories of strange physical portents. It would seem sensible, then, to take as our basis the earliest of the five, the narrative in St. Paul's letter to the Corinthian Church.

Furthermore, while St. Paul describes a series of appearances of the risen Christ to various persons, he includes in the list an appearance to himself; and he seems definitely to imply that all of them, including the one to himself, were of the same kind. Now we know what happened in St. Paul's case. He was on the road to Damascus, to help root out the Christian group in that city. Suddenly he saw a blinding flash and heard a voice which, he was quickly convinced, was the voice of Jesus. The experience left him dazed and ill. It seems to bear all the earmarks of an ecstatic vision. Since, then, St. Paul treats all the Resurrection appearances as of the same character, should we not regard them *all* as visions—God-inspired, if you like, but visions nonetheless? Many Christians have sincerely felt that this is the right answer; that Jesus' Resurrection was therefore a very real spiritual event, but not a physical one.

There are, however, some serious flaws in this theory.

Notice, first of all, to whom St. Paul was writing. The Corinthian Christians had been Greek pagans. Now such people would not have been perplexed over mere visions. They had known about visions all their lives, and it would have made no sense for St. Paul to argue with them on that score. Their problem was precisely that Christianity did *not* teach what they knew already, but something entirely strange to them. It was that unheard-of thing, that physical, historical thing, that St. Paul had to defend.

Second, all through his ministry and particularly with the Corinthians, St. Paul had to defend his right to be called an Apostle.[7] He based his right on the fact that Jesus had personally commissioned him, just as he had commissioned Peter and James and the rest. It would have done St. Paul's case no good whatever, to say that the other Apostles' *post*-Resurrection contacts with Jesus were, like his, mere visions. These other Apostles had known Jesus in the flesh (before his death, at any rate) and had been ordained by him. What St. Paul had to say, and did say repeatedly, was that his own meeting with the risen Jesus was real and bodily, like theirs:[8]

Am I not an apostle? am I not free? have I not seen Jesus our Lord?

He appeared to Cephas, then to the twelve . . . Then he appeared to James; then to all the apostles. And last of all he appeared to me also.

Third, St. Paul says that the risen Christ appeared 'to more than five hundred brethren at one time, of whom the greater part are alive unto the present.' Did any one ever persuade five hundred people to have the same

[7] Compare above, pages 136-41.
[8] I Corinthians 9:1; 15:5-8. That Paul had seen Jesus face to face may be implied, also, at II Corinthians 5:16.

vision at the same time, unless the 'vision' had a basis in physical reality?

Fourth, notice these phrases in St. Paul's account:

> 'He was buried,
> and the third day he rose again.'

For language to make sense, these two lines must be counterparts of one another. The second follows out of the first. It seems clearly to imply that St. Paul thought of a real emergence from the tomb.

Finally we must ask the question that was asked above, at the suggestion that the women found the wrong tomb. If Jesus' Resurrection appearances were visions and nothing more, why did not the enemies of Christianity produce his body? How could they miss this simplest of all ways to dispose of the hated religion? Is there any answer, any reasonable one at all, except that they could not, *because the body was not there?*

Thus every effort to explain the Resurrection away, or to make it other than what the Apostles said it was, becomes entangled in a maze of contradictions. Incredible as the Resurrection of Jesus may still seem, these proffered explanations are likewise incredible. They won't do.

Yet argument is not enough. There are still the thousands, the millions, who will face the Resurrection story sincerely, and sincerely turn away, saying, 'No, it cannot be. It does not fit my idea of God and the world.' To the man who feels thus, three things can be said. First, almighty God will no doubt have greater respect to one who honestly weighs the Christian claim and honestly rejects it, than to one who glibly repeats his creed, 'The third day he rose again from the dead,' without the awful import once catching in his mind.

Second, however, whether you or I believe the ancient

story or not, it is plain that the early Christians did believe it. They *knew* it, with such certainty that they gave their lives for it. Had they not, there would never have been any Christianity.

Lastly, what is 'my idea' of God? Is not God greater than my idea of Him? Is 'my' or 'our' mold certainly the right mold? Two thousand years ago a band of men, with the priceless boon of personal association with Jesus in the flesh, sought to fit him to their mold. He did not fit. Their mold was shattered, never to be put together again. Henceforth they must not mold, but be molded. There is our parable, and our lesson. The Christian—let it be said gently, but positively—the Christian is not fully Christian until he has seen the petty inadequacy of his own framework into which he would have compressed the truth of Christ. When he has seen that, then of a truth he can say with the Apostles of old, 'That I may know him, and the power of his Resurrection, and the fellowship of his suffering, being made comformable unto his death . . . God hath raised him from the dead, whereof all we are witnesses.'

CHAPTER XXII

THE CHRISTIAN ANSWER

For months, perhaps years, the disciples had lived, hiked, preached, eaten, slept out under the stars, in the company of the greatest man the world has ever known. Now he was gone from them, and yet he was not gone for his spirit moved them still.

Henceforth their lives were transfigured. They had been ordinary men, fishermen, tax-collectors or—at least one of them—rebels against the Roman government. They had been content to ply their trades, or had been excited in seeking Israel's freedom. Now this man had seized them. He had burned into their lives the memory of his words and deeds, and of his last and greatest deed. They knew, now, that he was the Lord's Messiah. So tax-collecting and fishing and agitating fell to one side. From now until their last breath they must tell about *him.* All of them would now have echoed the words of St. Paul, 'I determined not to know anything save Jesus Christ and him crucified. . . . Woe is me if I preach not the Gospel!' (*I Corinthians 2:2; 9:16*)

How should they go about it? What instrumentality was available, whereby they might broadcast their message? There was, of course, nothing resembling the modern newspaper or magazine. Books could be published, and would be in time, but this must be done by hand and the process was slow and cumbersome—much too slow and cumbersome for their present urgency.

One instrumentality was ready to hand. It was the synagogue. Synagogues offered two very great advantages. First, they were everywhere, since Jewish people had settled all around the Mediterranean Sea. Second, in getting speakers for the Sabbath services, synagogue organization was rather informal and flexible.[1] When an apostle came to town, evidently bearing a burning report about Israel's hoped-for Messiah, there was a very good chance that he would be invited to speak in the synagogue.

Well here you are, a young Christian apostle. Either you knew Jesus personally, or you have learned about him and been converted to his cause. Your trade used to be tent-making or fishing or farming. You may still have to summon back that skill in order to support your body, but your mind and your life are under greater commission. You will go throughout Palestine, or you will leave there and make for Egypt, Asia, Greece, Italy or Spain, wherever a synagogue will give you a hearing.

You come, say, to the city of Philippi. If you are wise you will procure lodging as close to the synagogue as possible, next door if you can, or up the street. You deposit your few belongings, then go and make yourself known to the ruler of the synagogue. Then, on Saturday, you go to the synagogue service. At the proper moment the ruler beckons you to come forward, it may be to read the Law or the Prophets, then certainly to expound. You stand before the congregation, their eyes fixed on you. You begin to speak. You take as your text a part of the Scripture that was just read. You say that that Scripture has been fulfilled in Jesus of Nazareth. You present Jesus to

[1] Above, pages 102ff.

your Jewish hearers as their long-awaited Messiah, the
answer to their and their fathers' hope.

Down in the congregation are several sorts of people.
One group is small. It consists of Jews who, like yourself,
have lived in Palestine and only lately come to Philippi.
Perhaps they recently moved here, or have come on
business or for a pleasure trip—travel was easy under
the Roman Empire. These people are few in numbers
but, as you know well, they are not weak. At first they
hear you with interest. Then, as your tale of a humiliated
and executed Messiah unfolds, their attention changes
to distaste, antagonism, and horrified revulsion. They will
stop you if they can. They may not interrupt the present
service, but they will murmur and put their hands to
their ears. Later they will try, by every means at their
disposal, to have you enjoined from repeating your damnable blasphemy. Even while you are speaking you are
aware that they may succeed; for others like them, in
other cities, have got people like you whipped or imprisoned or driven out of town. But, sometimes, they have
failed.

There is a second group. These too are Jews, like the
first group and like yourself. They too are loyal to their
faith, and they despise what you are saying. There is,
however, a difference. Unlike their friends from Palestine,
this second and larger group were born here in the Gentile world. Though brought up as strict Jews, they have
nevertheless rubbed shoulders with Gentiles all their
lives. They have learned something about Greek philosophy, and have observed other non-Jewish modes of thinking and living. Not all of it, they have discovered, is evil.
They realize that there are more things in heaven and
earth than their Palestinian cousins have seen. They will
join the Palestinians, certainly, in detesting and opposing

you. Yet a few of them may turn out to be just a bit broader of mind, a bit more willing to listen and to let you be heard.

There is a third group. Again they are Jews and loyal to the Law of Moses. These, however, are very different, for they were not always Jews. They are converts out of paganism, and are called 'proselytes.'

We have seen how the problem of death lay like a pall over the minds of young, intelligent pagans.[2] Sometimes they had sought for an answer in a reinterpreted mythology. There were myths of the gods and goddesses of Mt. Olympus coming down in the guise of men and women (and of animals) and consorting with human beings. There was even a myth, and it was widely known, of a dying and rising saviour god. It seems to have originated in the Orient. At an early period it was the basis of a widespread annual festival. The king or tribal chief would act out the part of the god. On a certain day in Spring he would present himself to the priests, submit to most revolting indignities, and disappear for a time. Then he would reappear, resplendent and garlanded with flowers, to depict the god's rising again.

Or, as we saw, the inquiring pagan might try philosophy, or this or that mystery cult. At best, however, it was all speculative. At worst it was silly and repulsive.

Into this sorry Gentile world Judaism had come. It seemed an absurd religion, with its forbidding initiatory rite and the uncouth Greek of its Scriptures. But its God was real, personal, close at hand and deeply concerned for the moral response of His children. It had a helpful and sustaining worship. In a most inspiring way, it filled its followers with fierce and unyielding loyalty. Judaism had much to give. Many a Greek man and still more

[2] Above, pages 122ff.

· 223

women overcame their revulsion and their laughter, and became Jews.

Now mark what you are saying to *them*. Less steeped in the lore of Israel, these hearers are less squeamish when you talk about this Messiah. Far more significantly, from their standpoint, your words offer to the proselytes everything they have found in Judaism—and more! Here is a solution to the problem of death that not Judaism nor any other faith can match. Here is a Being with whom man's life may *really* merge, and who, unlike Isis or Mithra, was actually in man's midst just a little while ago.

Implicit in this Christian answer is a claim. It is so unique that it could not have come from imitating other cults, but only from deepened understanding of Christ himself. It is so vast that no other religion, none whatever, has dared to make it. Indeed, the Church itself did not sense its full purport, nor make the claim explicit, until decades had passed. Finally it did so, and thereby spoke the greatest paradox of them all. Other religions told of gods coming in the *guise* of man or beast, magically taking or shedding this or that appearance. Or else they pictured human heroes who achieved divine honors and got themselves worshipped. Christianity would have none of such appearances and apotheoses. It offered, instead, the divine One who in fact *became* man, and eternally thus remains.

Other religions offered legends about deities. Christianity offered a *person* of recent and vivid memory. Others had imagined a dying and rising saviour god. The world's dying and rising Saviour God, said Christianity, is a man —not just an abstract or ideal man, but *this* man, *here*.

This, then, is what you are telling these proselytes as you stand before them: 'Your intuitions, in your pagan state, were true, and good. Your yearnings were valid yearnings, put into your mind by the Eternal Himself. But their fulfilment is not where you had looked, and it is not in a Judaism that knows not Christ. Their fulfilment is in Jesus who is the Christ.' After you are done, some of these proselytes will gather about you. 'We would hear more of this matter,' they will say.

Also listening to you is a large group of God-fearers.[3] These cannot bring themselves to undergo circumcision, but they have been otherwise strongly attracted to the Jewish religion. Many of them observe the Sabbath, keep the dietary laws, celebrate the Passover and the other feasts, and worship at the synagogue. Like their proselyte friends, but perhaps with even greater enthusiasm and sense of release, they welcome what you say and wish to learn more.

Finally there are the visitors and the curiosity seekers and the passers-by who just happened to drop in. Some of these, likewise, will be affected by your words. After the service they too may gather around you with the God-fearers and the proselytes, wishing to pursue the subject further. You invite them all to your lodging, not for today which is the Sabbath, but for tomorrow, Sunday. You may be denied this opportunity to talk with them again, for you have made strong enemies. Perhaps this time, however, you are to be more fortunate.

Let us say that you are fortunate. They come, and they listen. You enlarge upon your story of the day before, and you explain more fully whom you believe this man to be. The next Sunday they are back again, and the next. Presently there is a regular group, and it has grown so large that your modest dwelling will not house

[3] Compare above, pages 137f.

it. You borrow the home of one of your new-found friends.[4] There your people meet week after week or, because of their enthusiasm, day after day. You baptize them. You lay your hands upon their heads, just as all the Apostles have done wherever converts were made, and you say, 'Receive the Holy Spirit!' They have become a parish, one more cell in the life of the burgeoning Church.

You stay with them a few weeks, it may be, or a few months or a few years. You preach to them, and you work with them. You try to free them from the depraved morality of the surrounding life and establish them in a new and purer way. In your preaching and teaching you often recall, by way of illustration, sayings and incidents from the life of the Lord Jesus.

Illustrations for sermons and lectures are not the only occasions when you recall anecdotes about him. In any congregation problems will arise, some trivial, others serious, and you meet them with words and deeds which you remember from your Master's ministry. Mrs. Papadopoulos brings her baby to church. The baby cries, and some of the people complain. So you tell them that Jesus once said, 'Suffer the little children to come unto me, and forbid them not; for of such is the Kingdom of Heaven.' Or Mr. Papadopoulos and Mr. Demetrios have a quarrel. They lay it before you. You remind them of the word of the Lord, 'If thou art offering thy gift at the altar, and there rememberest that thy brother hath aught against thee, go: first be reconciled to thy brother, and then come and offer thy gift.' [5]

In such ways, as occasion demands, your congregation

---

[4] St. Paul referred frequently to 'the church which is in So-and-so's house': I Corinthians 16:19; Colossians 4:15; Philemon 2.
[5] See Matthew 19:13-15 = Mark 10:13-16; Matthew 5:21-26.

learns of incidents from his life, and comes to know his
pungent sayings and brilliant parables. Yet there is one
story you never tell like that. It is the story that gave you
your reason for being here. It is your gospel, seared into
your soul, and you recount it again and again, as a
single whole, and mostly in the same words. It is the
story of Jesus' death and resurrection.

In your congregation, one young man has been excep-
tionally stirred by all these anecdotes about Jesus. He
jots them down. Also he writes the record of the Passion
as you have told it so often. Years later, after you have
left, perhaps after you are dead, he gathers the stories
together. He is not always sure how they should be arranged, except for the obvious sequence of birth, boyhood, baptism, ministry, death, resurrection. Within that
broad framework he does his best. But the anecdotes are
like beads on a string: often he could have changed their
order drastically without much affecting the sense. Finally
he issues his collection as a book. It is a Gospel.

We can prove that that is how the stories of Christ were
put together. Open a New Testament to one of the
Gospels (*Mark* is the simplest) and examine it. About
two-thirds of it consists of just such little sayings and
anecdotes as we have described. Often they could be
completely rearranged without much altering the total
impression. They are, indeed, like disconnected beads on
a string. In the last part of the Gospel, however, that
feature is no more to be seen. Instead there is a long,
unbroken account of the events that led up to Jesus'
death, and then of that death and the events which followed. Here are no detached incidents, but a single whole.
Or take a *Book of Common Prayer* and look at the Epistles
and Gospels for the various Sundays and holy days. In
nearly every case the Epistle selection is obviously from

a longer context and one senses that it is an excerpt. Not so with the Gospel selections. These are, almost without exception, complete in themselves and comprise entire events, or parables or groups of sayings. The reason is plain: that is how the Gospel stories were told in the first place. That is how Christianity was first proclaimed.

One night as the disciples rowed over the lake, they saw Jesus walking toward them.[6] 'They all saw him,' says Mark, yet some were frightened and thought him a ghost. Again today, in proclaiming the ancient faith, we sometimes ride a sea of human knowledge and, still more, human explanations. At times, when he comes to us on that sea, we too may think him a spectre, a phantom of historical guess-work for whom none but a fool would wager his life. Or we may have believed him once but, when we saw the waves, like Peter we grew afraid and began to sink. Indeed, we must be afraid, until we listen. For across the waters of today's New Testament study there comes again a voice, authentic, clear, and which alone gives meaning and high value to the life of man. It is the Christian answer; and it is the only answer, the only proof the Christian has for all that he believes: 'Be not afraid. It is I.'

[6] Matthew 14:23-33; Mark 6:47-52; John 6:16-21.

CHAPTER XXIII

THE MAN CHRIST JESUS

Have you ever set out to describe something very familiar to you—an oak tree, say, or a paper clip? Have you tried to say what a friend looked like—and found that while his face was vivid in your mind, your words would fit any of a dozen persons? What is true of physical objects is even more true of intangible things. It would be hard to tell some one, who had never felt pain, what pain is. We all have friends, but how many could say clearly what friendship is? or anger, or boredom, or curiosity?

In the field of spiritual concerns, the task is most difficult of all. Most of us know (or think we know) what *religion* is; yet the world is still waiting for a satisfactory definition of it. Here are Christianity with its one God, polytheism with many gods, and Confucianism that officially has no god at all; Roman Catholicism with sacraments and elaborate ritual, and Quakerism that has neither; animism which worships material things, and Christian Science which denies that material things exist! All of these are religions, so that a good definition of 'religion' must fit them all.

Again, most of us know (or think we know) what *Christianity* is. Well, pick a hundred people at random and ask them to define it! There will be a variety of replies.

(1) Some will think of Christianity as a set of beliefs, or a philosophy of life. This type of answer is particularly likely to come from young people, who are themselves in search of a satisfying philosophy of life.

They will have much on their side. There *is* a distinctive Christian way of looking at things. The world, Christianity says, is like *this* and it is not like *that*. The world is a creation, produced by a God who knew what He was doing, cared what He did, and still cares. He cares so much that He asks for (but will not force) a personal response from us. His material world is sacred. Yet there is a spiritual world too, and no person can ever be, as was said of Kipling's vampire, just 'a rag and a bone and a hank of hair.' Physique and spirit are, in deepest reality, inseparable. Certainly there is a Christian world view, and its consequences are enormous.

While, however, Christianity *has* a philosophy, we may not say that it *is* a philosophy. If the Christian man's convictions are strong—so strong that sometimes he says, 'Here I stand. God helping me, I can do no other!'—there is a solid ground for those convictions, a foundation more firm than philosophy or creed. The real basis of Christian belief is not argument, cogent and useful as that may be. It is not the authority of the Church or the Bible, imposing and beloved as these may be. *It is a man.* The Christian looks at that man, and finds in him all that humanity has aspired to and longed for. Then, if he is true to his faith, the Christian does not say, 'I know what I believe.' He says, 'I know *whom* I have believed, and am persuaded that he is able to keep that which I have committed unto him.' [1]

(2) Others will maintain that Christianity is a way of

---

[1] II Timothy 1:12. A variant reading is, '. . . keep that which he hath committed unto me.'

behaving, or a way of life. They too will have much to bolster their contention. Phrases like 'Christian behavior,' 'un-Christian behavior' carry meaning to nearly all our minds. Many a time a minister or a layman hears some one say, 'Why should I go to church? Church people are no better morally than anybody else.' Whether the accusation is true or not (and it almost certainly is not) it shows how the outsider instinctively applies an ethical test to the Christian religion. Christians ought to behave better, be kinder, more unselfish, more sincere, purer, simply because they are Christians.

Yet noble as the Christian way of life is (or ought to be) this still does not get us to the heart of the matter. The fact is that nearly every ethical teaching in the New Testament has a parallel in other religions.[2] Long before Christ came the Hebrew people had learned and told of a God of righteousness. If His first word to them at Sinai was, 'I am the Lord thy God,' His second was, 'Thou shalt.' Christians sometimes cite, as a veritable summary of their religion, Jesus' saying, 'Thou shalt love the Lord thy God with all thy heart . . . and thy neighbor as thyself.' Jesus, however, was quoting Deuteronomy and Leviticus![3] True, he brought the two precepts together, whereas in the older books they are buried amid much that to us seems trivial. True also, it is Jesus' words that have echoed down the centuries. Nevertheless, long before he was born the world had learned much about loyalty and duty, and kindliness and forgiveness.

A further point must be made. To behave in a Christian way is not simply to obey this or that injunction. To behave like a Christian means *to be like Christ*. Once more, a *man* underlies the Christian teaching, and it is that

[2] Compare above, pages 6f.
[3] Matthew 22:34-40; Deuteronomy 6:5; Leviticus 19:18.

man who alone gives meaning to the Christian manner of life. Therefore we may not say that Christianity *is* a system of morals, but only that it *has* a system of morals. The basic Christian verb is not an imperative, 'Thou shalt.' It is an indicative, '*He came.*'

(3) Take any other description, or take anything we have said about Christianity in this book. No matter how true it is—indeed, to the extent that it is true—it carries us back to this person. Is Christianity the religion of the New Covenant, the new Israel, the beloved community? The covenant was sealed by that man. The Christian community is so intimately entwined with his life that it calls itself 'the Bride of Christ,' and even, 'the Body of Christ.'

Is Christianity an eschatological religion? The Christian is confident of the future only because that man has made him confident. It is he whom the Christian calls King, Lord and Judge. It is he, the Christian says, who 'shall come again, with glory, to judge both the quick and the dead; Whose kingdom shall have no end.'

Christianity is a sacramental religion. Most hallowed of all its moments is the moment of Holy Communion. Yet the disciples would never have come to that upper room, had they not for months and years been under that man's spell. When in years to come they gathered again about the holy table, their memory was of that strange man upon his cross. The words they all heard were his words again, '*My* body . . . *my* blood . . . Do this in remembrance of *me.*'

Christianity *is* not a philosophy, and it *is* not a moral code. It *is* not a Church, or a sacrament, or a hope. It *has* all these and they are infinitely, yes infinitely, precious. But they all derive from the other fact, the overwhelming reality. Basically, essentially, Christianity is a man who lived. It is an event. It is a story. At this time, at this place, under these circumstances, before these eyewitnesses, *this thing occurred*. At this known moment of history, God was in Christ reconciling the world unto Himself. *Our message is Jesus Christ.*

It will help now if we borrow from Christian scholarship one more long word. It is *Christology*. It means the study of the person and attributes of Christ. Never suppose that it is a dry, technical discipline whose answers are to most of us a matter of indifference. Christology faces the possibility—be it only a possibility—that the Eternal God is hereabouts. Possibly, in the records of this man, are issues on which hinge mankind's eternal destiny, your destiny, my destiny. Therefore the question which Christology asks is the most urgent that you or I shall ever hear or read: Who was, who is, this man?

In part, and so far as mere words permitted, he answered it himself. New Testament students often inquire, 'Did Jesus claim to be the Messiah?' A better question would be, 'Was "Messiah" a big enough term for what Jesus did claim?' The answer to that is, No. 'Messiah' is a word of human language, and human language is devised to cover earthly things but cannot cover divine things. (Sometimes we forget that.) Next to the divine Name, 'Messiah' was the most hallowed term in Israel's language. It told a portion, but only a portion, of what Jesus knew himself to be.

To 'Messiah' was added the concept of the Suffering Servant. This too was a most sacred phrase. It summed up Israel's furthest understanding of her own nature, and of God's purpose, through her, for all humanity. 'Messiah' and 'Suffering Servant' say much. Indeed, they say all that Hebrew and Aramaic were capable of saying about him. Even together, however, they do not say it all.

So, from the beginning, he pressed his claim in other ways. 'Follow *me*,' he said, and, 'Come unto *me*.' The scene of the Sermon on the Mount is laid early in his ministry. Many people regard it as the charter of Christian life. Listen, then, to Jesus' words: 'Blessed are ye when men shall say evil against you for *my* sake . . . *I* am not come to destroy but to fulfil. . . . Ye have heard what was said to them of old, but *I* say unto you. . . . Many will say unto *me* in that Day, Lord, Lord.' So early he knew that he would come in glory and that men should call him Lord.

Messiah—Suffering Servant—Lord. When Jews read the Old Testament, 'Lord' had been their surrogate for the name of very God! And still the Church could not stop. Before the century was out Christians had called him heavenly Priest, Lamb of God, Judge of living and dead, King of Kings, Word of God. Ever the urge was to say more. If New Testament writers never quite asserted, in so many words, 'Jesus is God,' again and again these men, who were Jews, spoke of him in terms that Jews had reserved for the Most High only. 'Grace to you and peace from God our Father and the Lord Jesus Christ.' 'Of him, and through him, and to him, are all things.' 'All things were made by him.' 'In him all things consist.'

Later the Church did say, explicitly, 'He is God.' It is one of the astonishing facts of history that the doctrine of Christ Jesus' divinity came into Christianity quietly, unobtrusively, and was not a subject of debate until long after it was the content of the universal faith.

Suppose that we too say all these things about him, and say also this last and greatest thing, 'He is God.' Suppose that we exhaust the resources of our own and every tongue on earth, in seeking to describe his meaning. What, in fact, have we done? We have sought to catch in the words of human speech, in sounds we can vociferate or letters we can draw, that which is beyond all words. Every Christology is, in the last analysis, a confession of failure. For every Christology is an effort to define the limitless, to express the unutterable. Nowhere is Jesus' saying more suited to our state than here: 'When ye have done all, still say, We are unprofitable servants.' (*Luke 17:7-10*) Still we try. While there is life on this planet, men will try to tell each other what he means.

Every Christology is the Church's effort to explain to itself, and to those round about, what this man Christ Jesus was and is. But he came first, and the Christology came afterward. We must always be willing to test our beliefs about him by the facts about him, to our utmost ability to know the facts. Unless we do that, Christology is an absurd waste of time. Unless we do it, indeed, there is no good reason why we should come out with a Christian faith at all, rather than with some other known or hitherto unknown doctrine.

Christianity is bound to the facts about Jesus. Some people wish that that were not so, and are tempted to deny that it is so. For suppose a historian should come along and prove that it all never really happened! Yes, let it be said now as we said at the beginning, the Christian takes a risk. With at least the devotion and loyalty he would give his spouse or his child, he wages his life in the belief that his Master is true. That is what St. Paul meant when he called himself 'Paul, a slave of Jesus Christ,' and when he said, 'For me, to live is Christ,' and, 'It is no longer I that live, but Christ liveth in me.' [4]

We might be proved wrong? The Christian knows that he will not be proved wrong. He knows his Lord, and seeks to know him more. His acquaintance cannot be like

[4] Romans 1:1; Philippians 1:21; Galatians 2:20.

the acquaintance of Peter, who strolled with him and sat by the lake in his presence, and who declared, 'Lord, I am ready to go with thee both to prison and to death,' and, 'Him God raised up the third day, and showed him openly. It is he which was ordained of God to be the Judge of living and dead.' [5] Yet if we cannot know him as Peter did, we still may watch him and trace his ways—

Here he begins in Galilee, the heavenly Voice reëchoing through his mind. There a crowd in a synagogue, or on a hillside, or by the lake, thrills at his words. Yonder he stands, his compassion for the uncertain throng as piercing as for a single lonely soul. The ostracized are his friends. So are the children. So, strangely, are some of the great or near-great. A madman meets him and finds sanity. A woman finds new health. The teachers of the Law charge him with sorcery. Yet so eminent he stands, that those who know him best are the first to name him Messiah. Then watch him as with resolution he turns from the popular idea of it, and sets his face toward Jerusalem and the end. His yearning compassion was always coupled with an imperiousness that baffled his friends. Now imperiousness and compassion surge up together as he enters the Holy City. See with what mastery he refutes his would-be examiners. Feel the deepening gloom, as the clouds of enmity gather head, and burst upon him in a storm of hatred, abuse and violent death. The verdict of history does not stop there. Soon we see his erstwhile followers hurtling from their hovel of despair, and here they are, there, everywhere, proclaiming that this Jesus is alive again, that they have been with him, that he shall live for ever and ever. And the central figure in all those pictures is no figment of unguarded imagining. It is the man Christ Jesus.

[5] Luke 22:33; Acts 10:36-43.

If we may not know him as Peter did, we may know him as Paul did. For Paul, like ourselves, came to him late and from a distance. It was not Peter but Paul (*Philippians 2:5-11*) who said,

'Have this mind in you, which was also in Christ Jesus: who, existing in the form of God, counted not the being on an equality with God a thing to be grasped, but emptied himself, taking the form of a servant, being made in the likeness of men; and being found in fashion as a man, he humbled himself, becoming obedient even unto death, yea, the death of the cross. Wherefore also God highly exalted him, and gave unto him the name which is above every name; that in the name of Jesus every knee should bow, of things in heaven and things on earth and things under the earth, and that every tongue should confess that Jesus Christ is Lord, to the glory of God the Father.'

INDEX